christmas
magic

Kate Shirazi

Photography by Emma Solley

PAVILION

First published in the United Kingdom in 2012 by
Pavilion Books
Old West London Magistrates Court
10 Southcombe Street
London, W14 0RA

An imprint of Anova Books Company Ltd

Design and layout © Pavilion, 2012
Text © Kate Shirazi, 2012
Photography © Pavilion, 2012

Commissioning editor: Emily Preece-Morrison
Designer: Georgina Hewitt
Photography: Emma Solley
Food stylist: Kate Shirazi
Copy editor: Kathy Steer
Indexer: Patricia Hymans

ISBN 978-1-86205-972-6

A CIP catalogue record for this book is available from the British Library.

10 9 8 7 6 5 4 3 2 1

Reproduction by Dot Gradations Ltd, United Kingdom
Printed and bound by SNP Leefung Printers Ltd, China

www.anovabooks.com

Contents

Introduction

When I think of Christmas, two clear memories spring to mind: firstly, waking up in the middle of the night, knowing it was far too early to think about putting the light on. Pushing a toe, I would feel a knobbly weight at the end of the bed. A little more toe wiggling would elicit the most wonderful rustling and crackling sound – the sound of a very stuffed sock. It would have been one of Dad's, chosen for maximum length and capacity. Father Christmas would have done some good work indeed. Much could be gleaned from an investigation with the feet from beneath the blankets. A comic would be poking out of the top and there would be the slight whiff of a novelty soap and maybe a sign that Father Christmas had been to a joke shop – whoopee cushions were big business in our house. Memory number two is far more applicable to this book – the feasting! Proper, no holds barred gluttony. The two biscuit rule disappeared for a day. There would be cake as well as the obligatory box of assorted biscuits. We knew it was good because there were biscuits after breakfast, crisps before lunch, multiple desserts, tea and then supper too, quite possibly followed by chocolates. If you didn't go to bed feeling mildly unwell, you hadn't done a proper job.

These days, I am less keen on the stuff-it-all-in-in-one-day approach to feasting, but I am still very concerned about the food on Christmas Day being spectacularly delicious. I suspect my calorie intake is much worse than all those years ago because, in fact, I extend the feasting by many days. Instead of the one big blow out, I do rather enjoy lots of smaller samplings. There may be drinks parties, lunches with friends, dinners with family, Boxing Day picnics (a bit of a tradition for us) and general high quality grazing over the period of about 10 days.

Shopping for ingredients

Christmas food should be special; out of the ordinary. In my world, far more important than the calorie count, is the "is this what I really, really want to eat?" factor. The joy of Christmas cooking is that the house smells headily delicious with never-ending wafts of cinnamon, clove and ginger, mingling with roasting meat, red wine, oranges and the foresty, pine whiff of the Christmas tree. Heaven.

I cannot pretend that Christmas feasting is cheap. When I shop, I do want value for money, but would rather have a really splendid, but smaller piece of meat than a larger, inferior one. I want any turkey, goose, cow or pig that gets scoffed to have had a decent life and a decent end. The huge chest freezers in the supermarket full of plastic wrapped giant frozen turkeys make me feel like having a small weep. Those birds are cheap, really cheap; too cheap. They haven't been reared or fed properly, and, after their demise, have been pumped full of water. I don't want to be involved in any part of that. The turkey I buy will come from a proper butcher who can tell me where the turkey comes from. Indeed, generally when I order my turkey, it is still wandering around a field blissfully ignorant of some woman in a butcher's shop signing its death sentence. It will be so good that not only will we eat it on Christmas Day, but also there will be lots of leftover meat, which will be fought over, and the bones will make the most delicious soup. We will eat the whole thing. I use the very same argument with whatever meat I buy. Buy less, buy better and eat the whole lot. Yum.

My next rant is about eggs. You know what's coming ... please, please buy free-range eggs. Hens should never be kept in cages. Hens are intelligent, funny creatures that do us a great service by laying eggs. They don't even try to bite you when you remove the eggs. Putting them in cages for a cheaper egg is wrong on so many levels. Wrong, you hear me? Wrong.

Organization

When it comes to Christmas cooking, my top tip is: don't drive yourself mad. If you want to make everything and will enjoy making everything, go ahead. No one will think any less of you if you buy marzipan instead of making it or stash some shop-bought shortcrust pastry in the freezer – it's really good; don't even think of making your own filo (phyllo) pastry. That way madness lies. I never make my own puff pastry. All butter puff pastry from a shop is consistently better than anything I make myself and I also don't like the harsh reality of seeing quite how much butter is involved. I really love cooking but I want to cook what I want to cook, especially at Christmas. Stand up for your rights and don't let anyone bully you into making cranberry sauce if you'd rather buy a jar. Life is too short.

Every year I am flabbergasted by the panic buying that goes on at the supermarket during the two days before Christmas. Shops are shut for one day. Yes, just the one day – at a push, two. It is like Armageddon is coming and all provisions that will be eaten in the shelters of doom will be of very high quality and frankly, too perishable. Candles, batteries and canned goods are needed in panic situations, not Stilton, smoked salmon and cream. Having said that, batteries are crucial unless you want to see some crumpled, wobbly chinned faces when you realize that "batteries are not included". Buy what you need, when you need it. With a more thought-out approach to Christmas food shopping, the bills really don't escalate out of control and the jars of weird stuff in cognac that seemed essential in the supermarket can stay on the shelf and out of your trolley. This is where lists are crucial. I love a list. I cannot pretend that I don't deviate from the list. I defy anyone not to, but with a list, you do actually manage to get what you require in the correct quantities.

The only thing left to say is get the carols on the radio, have a slug of the sherry and Happy Christmas Cooking!

The basics

To be honest with you, this chapter contains the recipes that are easy to make, but if you are having a time crisis or issues with confidence or would rather do something else altogether, all of these recipes can be found, ready made, in the supermarket. This is not to say that you shouldn't make them. Oh no. Homemade pastry, brandy butter and mincemeat are always going to be better than shop-bought stuff. You can have a fiddle with flavours and consistencies and really make them your own. And a kilner jar full of freshly made brandy butter, or juicy, fruity homemade mincemeat makes a lovely present.

The thing to remember when making pastry is the resting time in the refrigerator. Yes, I know it's boring, but it is crucial. The pastry really won't be as delicious and will almost certainly misbehave in the rolling out department if you neglect to chill the dough properly. Sorry. And if you are making sweet, flaky or shortcrust pastry, why not make double and put half in the freezer? You will feel efficient and smug, a winning combination, in my book.

Buttercream

A very handy icing (frosting) that can be flavoured with just about anything you want: very strong coffee, cocoa, lemon, lime or orange juices and zests, rose water, Marmite – no. Not Marmite. It also freezes really well for up to a month.

✳ Makes enough for 12 cupcakes

225 g/8 oz/2 cups icing (confectioners') sugar, sifted
100 g/3½ oz/7 tbsp unsalted butter, softened
1 tsp vanilla extract (optional)
1–2 tsp milk or water (optional)

Pop the sugar, butter and vanilla extract, if using, into a large bowl and beat away until the mixture is light and fluffy. If it's a bit on the heavy side, add the milk or water and beat in. If it's too thin, add more icing (confectioners') sugar.

That's it.

Royal icing

Royal icing is the one that sets really hard. It is useful for covering cakes and is essential if you want to do some decorative piping on cakes or biscuits. If you are covering a large cake, you might want to make double the amount...

✳ Makes enough to ice (frost) about 24 cupcakes

2 large free-range egg whites
500 g/1 lb 2 oz/4⅓ cups icing (confectioners') sugar, sifted
2 tsp freshly squeezed lemon juice

Put all the ingredients into a freestanding mixer and beat for 5–10 minutes, or until the mixture is very white, smooth and standing in stiff peaks. If the mixture is really stiff add 1 tsp water at a time until you get the correct consistency. If it is too runny, add more icing (confectioners') sugar.

To store the icing, pop it in a plastic container, cover the surface with clingfilm (plastic wrap) to exclude any air and seal the container tightly. Keep in the refrigerator for a week.

Marzipan

Whether you love it or loathe it, marzipan shrieks "it's Chriiiiiistmaaaas" in the manner of Noddy Holder circa 1978. It's really not tricky – why not give it a go?

※ Makes 450 g/1 lb (enough for a small Christmas cake)

225 g/8 oz/2½ cups ground almonds
125 g/4½ oz/½ cup + 2 tbsp caster (superfine) sugar
125 g/4½ oz/½ cup + 2 tbsp icing (confectioners') sugar
1 large free-range egg
1 tsp lemon juice
1 tsp almond extract (optional)

I put the ground almonds and both the sugars into a food processor and give it all a big blast to get everything really smooth. This is an optional extra and you don't have to do this – just mix the almonds and sugars together.

In a large bowl, whisk the egg with the lemon juice and almond extract, if using, then tip in the dry ingredients. Mix well then knead in the bowl with your hands until you have a lovely smooth paste. Add more almond extract or icing (confectioners') sugar if the mixture is sticky, and more lemon juice, or a few drops of warm water, if it is too dry.

When the paste is very smooth, wrap in 3 layers of clingfilm (plastic wrap) and store it in the refrigerator for up to a week.

Shortcrust pastry

This is very easy, if you have a food processor, embarrassingly so. No excuse not to make your own really...

✳ Makes enough for
1 large 25-cm/10-in tart
or 12 mince pies

50 g/1¾ oz/3½ tbsp butter
50 g/1¾ oz/3½ tbsp lard or
white vegetable fat (vegetable shortening)
225 g/8 oz/scant 1⅔ cups plain (all-purpose) flour, plus extra for dusting
salt
a tbsp or 2 of very cold water

If you are not using a food processor, in a bowl, rub both the fats into the flour until the mixture looks like fine breadcrumbs and add the salt. Add the cold water a spoonful at a time and mix until you have a firm dough. When the dough has come together into a ball, turn it out onto a floured work surface and knead a few times. Wrap the dough in clingfilm (plastic wrap) and chill for at least 30 minutes before you use it.

If you are using a food processor, put the fats, salt and flour into the bowl and pulse until you get a breadcrumb consistency. With the motor running, add the water in a fine trickle until the dough forms a ball. Turn out onto the floured surface, knead, wrap and chill as above.

Flaky pastry

Yum, yum! Quick and easy, requiring low levels of skill and high levels of greed, it's my kind of pastry. Make double and freeze the leftover half for up to a month. You can thank me later.

✳ Makes enough to cover
1 large pie

250 g/9 oz/1⅛ cups butter
(frozen if possible)
500 g/1 lb 2 oz/3½ cups plain
(all-purpose) flour, plus extra
for dusting
½ tsp salt
a tbsp or 2 of very cold water

If the butter hasn't been frozen, make sure it is really solid from the refrigerator. Soft is the enemy here. Put the flour and salt into a large bowl and grate the butter onto it. Yes grate. Then, with as few rufflings as you can manage, quickly incorporate the shavings of butter into the flour. The aim here is not to break up the butter, let it melt or become great globs, but to coat each shaving in flour. Slowly add enough water to turn the floury butter into a soft dough.

When the dough comes together, turn it out onto a floured work surface and knead it gently, then quickly wrap it in clingfilm (plastic wrap) and rest in the refrigerator for at least half an hour. You should clearly be able to see the shards of butter in the pastry.

Sweet pastry

A delicious tart for dessert needs to be made with sweet pastry. It might look like a bit of a faff if you aren't really into pastry-making. Believe me when I say it is the work of five minutes and is one of the best-behaved pastries that I have ever come across.

✳ Makes enough for
  1 large 20-cm/9-inch tart
  or 12 little ones

175 g/6 oz/¾ cup unsalted
  butter
50 g/1¾ oz/¼ cup caster
  (superfine) sugar
250 g/9 oz/1¾ cups plain (all-
  purpose) flour, plus extra
  for dusting
pinch of salt
1 large free-range egg yolk
about 1 tbsp very cold water

I do all of this in a food mixer, but it's entirely up to you. Firstly, cream the butter and sugar together until lovely and pale. Add 1 tbsp of the flour and beat in, then add the egg yolk and beat in. Add the flour 1 tbsp at a time, beating well between each addition then add the water to bring the dough together.

Tip the dough onto a floured work surface and knead quickly until it forms a smooth ball. Wrap the dough in clingfilm (plastic wrap) and chill in the refrigerator. I leave this dough for at least an hour before I use it, but longer if possible.

Brandy or rum butter

Yes, you can buy this in containers, but homemade is infinitely nicer. You can alter the strength and sweetness to suit your palate – and your dessert. A lighter Christmas pudding doesn't need a hedge slammer of a brandy butter. No, it requires a fluffier, paler, whisper of a butter. Conversely, a dense, dark, sticky pudding needs a heftier butter. See what I mean?

✳ Enough for 8 quite greedy people

225 g/8 oz/1 cup unsalted butter
225 g/8 oz/2 cups icing (confectioners') sugar, sifted
2–3 tbsp rum or brandy
finely grated zest of 1 orange (optional)
2 tsp lemon juice (optional)

Beat the butter really well until is it super pale and soft, then beat in the sugar. When the sugar is fully incorporated add the rum or brandy very slowly, while beating all the time. This stops the butter "splitting". Keep tasting (poor you) and stop adding the alcohol when either you fall over or you like the taste. Add the orange zest and lemon juice if you want a zingier version.

Put the butter in a jar, seal well and keep it in the refrigerator for up to a week. You can also freeze it for up to a month.

My favourite mincemeat

This is a lighter, fruitier and, dare I say, less turgid, version of the traditional mincemeat. It is contains no suet at all (beef or vegetable) and putting your nose in jar of this is like inhaling Christmas. Use this recipe as a base and add whatever dried fruit, spices, flavours and alcohol you wish: dried cranberries, coriander seeds, and crystallized (candied) ginger have all been added at one time or another.

I give a final weight indication here rather than specifying number of jars as all jars are different. This recipe makes enough for all your mincemeat needs plus a few jars to give away as presents!

✳ Makes 1.8 kg/4 lbs

225 g/8 oz/1⅛ cups dark soft brown sugar
200 ml/7 fl oz/generous ¾ cup apple juice (cloudy preferably)
1 kg/2 lb 4 oz cooking apples, peeled, cored and chopped into small dice
1 tsp ground allspice
1 tsp ground cinnamon
225 g/8 oz/1½ cups currants
225 g/8 oz/generous 1⅓ cups raisins
50 g/1¾ oz/½ cup flaked (slivered) almonds
grated rind and juice of 1 lemon
2 tbsp brandy (optional)

Put the sugar and apple juice into the largest pan that you own and slowly dissolve the sugar in the juice, stirring occasionally. Then simply add everything else and any extras you have decided to use. Bring the mixture to the boil, reduce the heat and simmer for 30 minutes, stirring quite frequently to stop the mixture sticking.

Sterilize your jars either by heating them in the oven or putting them through a very hot wash in the dishwasher and ladle the mincemeat into the hot jars. Top with lids, but don't tighten the seals until the mixture is cool.

Savoury bites

2

I adore small food – that is food in miniature, not small quantities. My ideal meal would be a non-stop flow of canapés. Christmas is the time when I can thoroughly indulge my passion: the drinks parties, the people who drop in for a small snifter, the pre-meal snackette. There are endless, wonderful opportunities to whisk something out of the freezer and whack it in the oven for 10 minutes. Hey presto – a plate of small, savoury succulents. Somehow, this doesn't feel quite so right on a wet Tuesday lunchtime in February, but at any point of the day or night during the 12 days of Christmas, a little morsel (or five) of something rather exquisite is entirely appropriate. And the other bonus is, it really doesn't go so well with a cup of tea. No, a bottle needs to be opened. Mulled wine must not be drunk without a canapé of some sort. I'm sure I read somewhere that it could seriously damage your health, if you drank it without small food...

Just about everything in this chapter can be made ahead and frozen or kept sealed in a jar or container. There may be some minor last minute assemblage, but minor is the operative word here. Effortless entertaining with maximum effect – that's what we're aiming for.

Mildly exotic turkey patties on brioche buns

I say "mildly" exotic, because they are fresh and zingy tasting rather than powerfully spicy. Turkey mince (ground turkey) is wonderful. Order it from your butcher - it will be very different from the rather pallid, watery and sad stuff you can get in the supermarket. Both the buns (cooked) and the patties (uncooked) can be frozen and added to your stash of freezer wonderments.

✳ Makes about 20 small buns

For the brioche
15 g/½ oz fresh yeast
2 tbsp warm water
50 g/1¾ oz/3½ tbsp butter
225 g/8 oz/scant 1⅔ cups strong white bread flour, plus extra for dusting
1 tbsp caster (superfine) sugar
½ tsp salt
2 large free-range eggs, beaten
sunflower oil, for oiling
1 large free-range egg, beaten, to glaze

For the turkey patties
50 g/1¾ oz/3½ tbsp butter
4 shallots, finely chopped
2-cm/¾-in piece of fresh ginger, peeled and finely chopped
1 green chilli, finely chopped
1 garlic clove, crushed
450 g/1 lb turkey mince (ground turkey), preferably from the legs
(list continues opposite)

Crumble the fresh yeast into the warm water and stir it around until it has dissolved. Set aside and let it do its magic and start frothing (this will take about 15 minutes).

Melt the butter and cool slightly. Put the flour, sugar, salt, butter, beaten eggs and yeasty liquid into a large bowl and mix together to form a dough. Tip the dough onto a floured work surface and knead for about 10-15 minutes until the dough is smooth, silky and elastic. Put the ball of dough back in the bowl and score a deep cross in it. Cover with clingfilm (plastic wrap) and leave to prove (rise) for about 1 hour, or until doubled in size.

Oil 1 or 2 baking trays. Take the dough out of the bowl and knead it again for 5 minutes then divide the dough into 20 portions. Form each portion into balls and place them on the prepared baking trays, spaced well apart. Cover again with clingfilm and leave the brioche to prove once more. It is done when the dough looks light and puffy – depending on the warmth of your proving space, this will take between 30-45 minutes.

1 tbsp coriander (cilantro) leaves,
  finely chopped
salt and freshly ground black
  pepper
sunflower oil, for frying

To serve
any salsa, cranberry sauce, relish
  or mayonnaise that appeals

Preheat the oven to 230°C/450°F/Gas Mark 8 (yes, it is hot).

Brush the top of the buns with the beaten egg and bake for about 8–10 minutes, or until golden delicious. Try not to eat them all straight from the oven... If you are freezing them, pop them in a bag and put them into the freezer as soon as they are cold. They will keep for up to a month.

To make the patties, melt the butter in a frying pan (skillet) and gently sauté the shallots until they are soft, but not golden. Add the ginger, chilli and garlic and give everything a quick heat through.

Tip the turkey mince into a large bowl. Add the shallot mixture, coriander and a good pinch of salt and a few grinds of pepper. Mix everything together (I use my hands – so much easier). To test the flavour and seasoning, heat the frying pan again with a tiny smidgen of oil. Take a very small piece of the mince mixture and fry until it is cooked all the way through, then taste and add more seasoning if necessary. When you are happy, form the mince into small patties (bearing in mind the size of your buns) and either put them in the refrigerator for 1–2 hours until you want to fry them or freeze them straight away in their uncooked state, for up to a month.

To cook the patties, defrost if necessary, and shallow-fry them in hot oil for about 6–7 minutes on each side until cooked. To make sure that the meat is cooked all the way through cut one in half.

To serve, split a brioche bun in half and lightly toast it. Pop a pattie into the bun and top with a dollop of salsa, cranberry sauce or any other unguent that appeals. Delish.

Spinach filo cigars

The combination of spinach and cheese is a classic. In the summer I put in lots of fresh chopped herbs like mint and dill, but in winter use fennel seeds and nutmeg. These beauties freeze really well and can be cooked from frozen.

* Makes 40

1 kg/2 lb 4 oz bag frozen leaf
    spinach, defrosted
200 g/7 oz feta cheese
250 g/9 oz/generous 1 cup cream
    cheese or quark
2 large free-range eggs
1 tsp fennel seeds
1 tsp lemon thyme leaves
½ tsp freshly grated nutmeg
salt and freshly ground black
    pepper
250 g/9 oz packet filo (phyllo)
    pastry
250 g/9 oz/1⅛ cups butter,
    melted

* If you are going to freeze them, put them on a baking sheet in a single layer, uncooked, in the freezer. Once frozen, remove them from the tray and put into a plastic freezer bag and freeze until you would like to use them. You can cook them from frozen for about 30–35 minutes.

Preheat the oven to 180°C/350°F/Gas Mark 4.

Start by trying to extract as much water as possible from the spinach. A particularly satisfying method is to roll the spinach up in a clean tea towel and wring it out over the sink. Put the spinach into a large bowl and crumble over the feta. Add the cream cheese, eggs, fennel seeds, thyme and nutmeg and stir well so that everything is incorporated. Taste the mixture and add salt and pepper and more nutmeg to taste.

Put another clean tea towel under cold running water and wring it out, then put the filo (phyllo) pastry inside the towel so that it is completely covered in damp fabric. Take 1 sheet of filo and cut it in half lengthways, then cut each strip across widthways, so you end up with 4 pieces.

Brush the whole surface of one of the filo strips with melted butter then form 1 tsp of the spinach mixture into a sausage shape and put it at the top of the filo, leaving a 1 cm/½ in gap at the top and sides. Fold the sides in over the edge of the spinach and fold the rest of the length of the filo in too. Simply roll up the cigar and place it on a baking sheet (it doesn't need to be greased) and brush more butter over the top of the cigar. Repeat until you have used up all the mixture.

Bake in the oven for 25–30 minutes, or until the cigars are golden brown and deliciously crispy.

Kate's spicy nuts

A recipe so easy, it's criminal. Word of warning – these are very moreish, so if you are giving them as a present, seal the jar properly so you aren't tempted to break in and just "check" that they are still OK.

* Serves 8 for nibbles

50 g/1¾ oz/3½ tbsp butter
1 tbsp olive oil
3 tbsp runny honey
2 tbsp soy sauce
1½ tsp hot smoked paprika
1 tsp Maldon sea salt
400 g/14 oz/2⅔ cups mixed
    whole nuts (I used Brazils,
    almonds and cashews)

Preheat the oven to 140°C/275°F/Gas Mark 1 and line a baking sheet with silicone paper.

Put the butter and olive oil into a frying pan (skillet) large enough to take all the nuts comfortably. When the butter has melted, add the honey, soy sauce, paprika and salt and stir, letting the mixture bubble for about 30 seconds.

Tip all the nuts in and stir them very well so that all the nuts are covered in the lovely mixture.

Tip the whole caboodle onto the prepared baking sheet and roast in the oven for about 30 minutes, or until the nuts are deeply golden.

Leave the nuts to cool on the baking sheet. When they are completely cold, break them up a little and put them into kilner jars without "testing" too many on the way.

A brilliant present, but quite hard to give away...

Savoury scones

These mini morsels of wonderment are yet another doddle to make. Do feel free to add or subtract ingredients and flavours to suit your toppings. For instance, try a tablespoon of chopped fresh dill and chives to go with salmon and cream cheese, or perhaps a tablespoon of chopped artichokes from a jar and a few chunks of feta cheese to go with a smear of tapenade and some sun-blushed tomatoes ... you get the idea.

✳ Makes about 20 mini scones

50 g/1¾ oz/3½ tbsp butter, plus extra for greasing
225 g/8 oz/scant 1⅔ cups self-raising flour, sifted, plus extra for dusting
½ tsp salt
1 tsp baking powder
2 tsp English mustard powder
2 tbsp freshly grated Parmesan cheese
1 tbsp black olives, pitted and roughly chopped
150 ml/5 fl oz/⅔ cup milk
1 large free-range egg, beaten

Preheat the oven to 220°C/425°F/Gas Mark 7. Grease and flour 2 baking sheets.

In a large bowl, mix together the flour, salt, baking powder and mustard powder. Chop the butter into pieces and rub it into the flour until you get a breadcrumb consistency. Stir in the grated cheese and chopped olives (or whatever other flavours you are adding) then slowly mix in the milk – you may not need it all. Stop adding the milk when you have a soft dough that holds together.

Tip the dough out onto a floured work surface and knead gently. Gently is the operative word – don't knock all the air out. Lightly roll out the dough until it is about 2.5 cm/1 in thick and cut out circles. Place them onto the prepared baking sheets and brush their surfaces with the beaten egg.

Bake for 8–10 minutes, or until risen and golden. Transfer to a wire rack to cool before splitting them in half and topping with you chosen loveliness. These ones are delicious with mature (sharp) Cheddar cheese and a dollop of chutney.

Ricotta and smoked salmon mini muffins

Confession time: this recipe is extremely similar to one that I first wrote for *Cupcake Magic*. I include it here because: a) I really like it; b) it is easy peasy; c) it is quite festive and d) because I can.

* Makes 24 mini muffins or 12 regular-sized muffins

butter, for greasing (optional)
75 g/2¾ oz/½ cup plain (all-purpose) flour
100 g/3½ oz/⅔ cup polenta (cornmeal)
½ tsp salt
1 tsp baking powder
2 large free-range eggs, beaten
150 g/5½ oz/⅔ cup ricotta cheese
75 g/2¾ oz/⅓ cup butter, melted
4 large slices of smoked salmon, roughly chopped
2 tbsp chopped dill

To serve (optional)
Crème fraîche
Keta salmon caviar

Preheat the oven to 190°C/375°F/Gas Mark 5 and line a 24-hole mini muffin tin or a 12-hole muffin tin with paper cases (cups). Grease the tins if not using cases.

Sift the flour into a large bowl and add the polenta (cornmeal), salt and baking powder, giving it a good old stir. In a second bowl, mix together the eggs, ricotta and melted butter. Add the salmon and dill and stir again Tip the bowl of wet ingredients onto the dry ingredients and stir very briefly until it is just incorporated. Overstirring at this stage will result in heavy muffins. Words one never wants to hear.

Don't worry about the lumps, just spoon the batter into the prepared tins and bake for 10–15 minutes until the muffins are firm and golden and a skewer inserted comes out clean. If you are making larger muffins, you will need to bake them for at least another 5 minutes.

Take the muffins out of the tins and leave to cool on a wire rack. They are delicious eaten barely warm, with a dollop of crème fraîche and a smidgen of salmon caviar on top.

Blinis

I do love a blini. Oh yes. I will happily admit that for years I bought them in packets from the supermarket. Homemade? A revelation. Soft, full of flavour and moreish, not only are they a vehicle for so many scrumptious toppings, but homemade blinis are frighteningly delicious straight from the pan. Traditionally blinis contain yeast, but my super quick version does not. I'm not concerned by this, and hope you don't mind either.

✳ Makes about 20

170 g/6 oz/scant 1½ cups buckwheat flour
2 tsp baking powder
salt and freshly ground black pepper
290 ml/10 fl oz/1¼ cups whole milk
4 large free-range egg whites
butter, for frying

Sift the flour into a large bowl and stir in the baking powder, a pinch of salt and a couple of grinds of pepper. Add the milk and mix everything together until you have a smooth batter.

In a second bowl, whisk the eggs whites with a pinch of salt until the whites hold soft peaks. Then, with a metal spoon carefully fold the egg whites into the batter – I do this in 3 batches rather than all at once.

Melt the butter in a heavy-based frying pan (skillet) and when it is sizzling, drop little spoonfuls of the batter into the pan. The size of the blinis is really up to you. You can make them with teaspoons, dessertspoons – your choice.

When you see little bubbles come to the surface of the blini, it should be a golden brown underneath (have a peep to check), then carefully flip it over and cook for another 1–2 minutes until golden brown. Keep the blinis warm while you cook the rest of the mixture, adding more butter to the pan as needed.

Top the blinis with whatever you like: cream cheese, crème fraîche, salmon, smoked eel, caviar, spicy salsas and soft blue cheeses are all good.

Sausage rolls

Sausage rolls make me want to laugh. There is something undeniably naff about them. However a warm, homemade sausage roll is a force to be reckoned with, teasing its detractors with golden, herby, porky, buttery wafts. I think you will find that the naysayers change their tune rather...

✳ Makes 16 small sausage rolls

500 g/1 lb 2 oz packet all butter puff pastry
plain (all-purpose) flour, for dusting
2 tbsp mustard (grainy or smooth)
6 sage leaves, finely chopped (or thyme)
8 large sausages (go for an interesting sausage...)
1 large free-range egg, beaten

Roll out the pastry on a lightly floured work surface until you have a rectangle of about 50 x 30 cm/20 x 12 in. Cut the rectangle in half, then cut each half in half again. You should have 4 rectangles now. Cut each rectangle in half, and half again. You should now have 16 rectangles.

Spread a thin layer of mustard over each rectangle and a light smattering of chopped sage or thyme. Remove the sausages from their casings and chop each one in half.

Take a rectangle of pastry and put a sausage half at one end. Lightly dab the other end with a little beaten egg and roll up the sausage using the eggy end to stick the pastry together. Place onto a non-stick baking tray with the seam underneath and repeat until you have 16 little beauties. Put the sausage rolls in the refrigerator for at least 30 minutes to firm up. You can freeze them at this stage for up to a month, if you like.

When you are ready to cook them, preheat the oven to 180°C/350°F/Gas Mark 4.

Score the tops of the sausage rolls with a sharp knife and brush liberally with the beaten egg. Bake for 25–30 minutes, or until the pastry is puffed up and golden and the sausages are cooked all the way through. Leave to cool before scoffing.

Tiny pasties

Well, I say "tiny" but I don't mean "tiny". Who wants a tiny pasty? Not me. I want a proper mouthful. You just don't need two hands to eat one.

✳ Makes 12–15 small pasties

1 batch shortcrust pastry (see p.13), made with lard – not butter
450 g/1 lb beef (chuck is best)
1 large onion, finely chopped
90 g/3 oz swede (rutabaga) and carrot, peeled and chopped into 5-mm/¼-in dice
1 large baking potato, peeled and diced as above
½ tsp chopped thyme
salt and freshly ground black pepper
plain (all-purpose) flour, for dusting
1 large free-range egg, beaten

✳Make and chill the pastry as directed on p.13.

Preheat the oven to 200°C/400°F/Gas Mark 6. Remove all the skin and gristly bits from the beef and chop it as finely as you can. Mix together the meat, vegetables, thyme and a good large pinch of salt and lots of pepper.

Roll out the pastry on a floured work surface until it is about 5mm/¼ in thick. Use a teacup, glass or small saucer as a template to cut out circles and put 1–2 tsp of the beef filling (depending on the size of your circles) down the middle of the pastry. Brush the edges of the pastry with beaten egg and pull up the sides and stick them together, pinching and crimping the top as you go.

Make 2 small holes in the top of the pasty to let the steam escape and brush the whole surface with more beaten egg. Place the pasties on a baking sheet and bake for 20 minutes, before turning the oven temperature down to 170°C/325°F/Gas Mark 3 and baking for another 35–40 minutes, or until beautifully golden and the pastry is crisp.

Eat hot, warm or cold – one handed.

Smoked salmon tarts

Not many people turn their noses up at smoked salmon, but do substitute smoked trout if you prefer as it is equally delicious. You can also turn this into one large tart as well and have it for lunch with salad.

* Makes 12 small tarts

1 batch shortcrust pastry,
    see p.13
butter, for greasing
plain (all-purpose) flour,
    for dusting
200 g/7 oz/generous ¾ cup
    cream cheese
2 large free-range eggs, lightly
    beaten
150 g/5½ oz smoked salmon,
    roughly chopped
1 tbsp chopped dill
salt and freshly ground black
    pepper
lemon juice, to taste (optional)

* Make and chill the pastry as
    directed on p.13.

Preheat the oven to 160°C/315°F/Gas Mark 2–3. Grease a 12-hole muffin tin with butter.

Roll out the pastry on a lightly floured work surface to about 2mm/¹⁄₁₆ in, or as thin as you dare. Cut out discs of pastry and use to line the prepared muffin tin, being aware that you don't need the pastry to come all the way up the sides of the hollows – that would be one deep filled pie!

Fill each pastry case (shell) with scrunched up baking parchment and baking (dried) beans – or (there's a top tip coming here) put a paper muffin case on top of the pastry and tip the beans into this. Bake the pastry cases for about 15 minutes, or until the pastry is cooked all the way through. Remove the papers and beans and leave the pastry cases to one side. Turn the oven down to 140°C/275°F/Gas Mark 1.

Put the cream cheese into a bowl and beat to loosen it then tip in the salmon, eggs and dill and stir thoroughly. Season well and taste the mixture, adding the lemon juice if you think it needs it.

Carefully spoon the mixture into the pastry cases and bake for 15–20 minutes until the filling is just set. Leave the tarts to cool in the tin and eat warm or cold.

Stilton and pear tarts

These are tiny on purpose. They are rich beyond belief. I adore the sweet pear clashing with the salty Stilton, the crisp pastry, creamy filling and juicy fruit, finally the crunch of a walnut – my idea of heaven. You can make the pastry cases (shells) well in advance, as well as the filling – just make sure they only meet each other about an hour before serving.

* Makes about 30 tiny tarts

1 batch shortcrust pastry,
    see p.13
butter, for greasing
plain (all-purpose) flour, for
    dusting
2 large, ripe pears, quartered,
    cored and peeled
juice of 1 lemon
200 g/7 oz Stilton
1½ tbsp good mayonnaise
3 tbsp crème fraîche
1 tbsp finely chopped parsley
30 walnut halves

*Make and chill the pastry as
   directed on p.13.

Preheat the oven to 160°C/315°F/Gas Mark 2–3 and grease a mini muffin or tart tin with butter.

Roll out the dough on a floured work surface to about 2 mm/1⁄16 in thick and cut out discs of about 6 cm/2½ in. Push the discs into the prepared tin and prick them all over with a fork. Cover the dough with squares of baking parchment and weigh them down with baking (dried) beans. Bake the dough for about 10 minutes, or until cooked through.

Put the quartered pears into a saucepan of water together with the lemon juice and gently simmer until the pears are soft and tender. This can take anywhere from 5 minutes to 15 depending on the state and size of your pears. When they are cooked, drain and chop them into 5-mm/¼-in cubes.

Put the Stilton into a large bowl and mash it up with a fork. Add the mayonnaise and crème fraîche and mix everything up really well so that you don't have massive lumps of Stilton hanging around. Add the parsley and pears and gently fold everything in.

Take small teaspoons of the mixture and fill the pastry cases (shells). Top with a walnut and you are good to go.

The main event

3

Turkey and all the trimmings? Delicious, but too often the default setting. The truth is, there isn't actually a law that states you must plonk a massive roast bird onto the table along with 15 bowls of steaming vegetables, sauces, small meat products and condiments. The main event should be a feast, but it doesn't need to be a whole roast turkey if you feel like a bit of a change.

In my world the really crucial things that may never, ever be omitted are lots of roast potatoes, red cabbage, at least two other vegetables (which may be simple), bread sauce and some sort of vehicle for gravy. I don't actually care if it's turkey, goose, beef or a stew. For many, many years I didn't eat meat at all and so a nut roast was my Christmas dinner of choice. I got it down to a fine art and I include my recipe in this chapter.

Stuffed turkey breast

Easy to carve, there's no waste and it doesn't take all day to cook. Buy a whole turkey and get your butcher to mince the legs for you (see p.20) and bone the breasts. Keep the bones for making stock.

* Serves 6–8 depending on the original size of the bird

50 g/1¾ oz/3½ tbsp butter
1 large onion, finely chopped
450 g/1 lb really good herby sausages, skinned
200 g/7 oz cooked, peeled, ready to use chestnuts, chopped
3 rosemary sprigs, chopped (optional)
12 rashers (strips) smoked streaky (lean) bacon
2 turkey breasts (about 900g/ 2 lb each), skinned

* You will need string!

Preheat the oven to its highest setting.

Make the stuffing first. Melt the butter in a pan and sweat the onion until really soft but not brown. In a large bowl, mix together the sausagemeat, chestnuts and onion. If you want an extra herby kick, add the rosemary.

On a large flat surface, lay the bacon out into a neat sheet and place one of the turkey breasts in the middle (what would have been skin side down). Make a long sausage shape of the stuffing and place it down the centre of the breast, then put the other breast on top (what would have been skin side up). Carefully pull the bacon over the top of the turkey, giving it a bit of a pull as you go, so that it is tightly wrapped. Flip it over so that the bacon edges are underneath and tie it all up with string, to keep it shut.

Put the turkey on a roasting tray, pat it for luck and put it in the screamingly hot oven for 15 minutes. After which time, turn the oven down to 170°C/325°F/Gas Mark 3 and roast for about 1½ hours. If it looks like it is getting too brown and crisp, cover with foil. The meat is done when a skewer inserted into the very middle releases clear juices. Slightly pink – not done, put it back and try again in 15 minutes.

When the meat is done, take it out of the oven, wrap in foil and leave it somewhere warm to rest for 15–20 minutes before carving. This makes all the difference, believe me.

Roast potatoes

As far as I am concerned there are three main rules associated with roast potatoes. Number one: always cook at least 10 more than you think you will need. When you see "uses for leftover roast potatoes" I am genuinely puzzled. Leftover roast potatoes? I think not. Number two: they always take longer than you think to crisp up, therefore leave yourself lots of time to cook the beauties. Number three: use a decent potato. It needs to be floury (mealy), none of this new potato nonsense. I haven't used quantities here on purpose. Look at the size of the raw potatoes, decide how many people will eat and add a few more.

sea salt
potatoes
2 tbsp fat, such as sunflower oil,
    rapeseed oil, goose fat, duck fat
    or beef dripping

Preheat the oven to 180°C/350°F/Gas Mark 4, if it is not already on cooking your goose, or whatever else you've got in there.

Bring a large pan of water to the boil and add a little salt. Peel the potatoes and cut them into the size you want (whopper, middlies or delicates). Parboil them (this means, boil them for 10 minutes) and then drain them in a colander. Give the colander a good rattle and shake and you should see the edges of the potato get all roughed up and scruffy. This is very good. Smooth – not so good.

Put 2 tbsp fat into a roasting tin and put in the oven to heat up. When the fat is all shimmery and hot, hot, hot, carefully take it out and add the potatoes. Watch out for spitting. Turn the potatoes in the fat and sprinkle them with some sea salt then roast in the oven for at least 1 hour, turning them around in the tin every 20 minutes or so. They are done when they are deeply golden and so crispy on the outside they make you want to have a small weep.

Dauphinoise potatoes

There are so many versions of this delicious dish that I am just going to go with it and write down what I do. It isn't very authentic, so I'm sorry if I upset puritans. It works. It tastes jolly good and is gratifyingly bad for you.

✳Serves 6

1 kg/2 lb 4 oz potatoes (use floury/mealy ones)
salt and freshly ground black pepper
300 ml/10 fl oz/1¼ cups double (heavy) cream
300 ml/10 fl oz/1¼ cups milk
1 plump garlic clove, crushed
butter, for greasing
freshly grated nutmeg
75 g/2¾ oz/⅔ cup Gruyère cheese, grated

Preheat the oven to 160°C/315°F/Gas Mark 2-3.

Peel and slice the potatoes into circles about 3 mm/⅛ in thick. Bring a large pan of salted water to the boil and cook the potatoes for about 8 minutes, or until they are just tender when pierced with the point of a sharp knife. Drain them well then lay them out on clean tea towels or sheets of kitchen paper (paper towels) to soak up any starch.

In a large jug, mix together the cream, milk and garlic and a good amount of salt and pepper.

Grease a gratin dish well with butter and arrange the potatoes in layers in the dish, grating a small amount of nutmeg over each layer. Pour the creamy, garlicky liquid over the potatoes and then top with the grated cheese.

Put a layer of foil over the dish and bake for about 1 hour until the potatoes are really soft. Remove the foil, turn the oven up to 180°C/350°F/ Gas Mark 4 and cook, uncovered, for another 30 minutes until the top is golden and the cream is bubbling thickly around the edges.

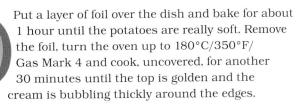

Our red cabbage

I watched my Granny make red cabbage this way. I watched my Mum make red cabbage this way. My sister and I also make red cabbage this way. I have never, ever seen anyone write it down anywhere. It was, I would like you to know, incredibly difficult to commit it to paper as it is so instinctive: a splash of this, a dollop of that. Agony, I tell you. Agony. This is a dish which is infinitely better eaten a couple of days after making – it freezes really well too.

* Serves 8

1 red cabbage (about 750 g/
   1 lb 10 oz)
1 tbsp vegetable oil
1 large onion, peeled and
   chopped
2 medium dessert apples or
   one cooking apple, peeled,
   quartered and sliced
4 cloves
3 bay leaves
3 tbsp dark soft brown sugar
4 tbsp red wine vinegar
350 ml/12 fl oz/1 ½ cups water
salt and freshly ground black
   pepper

Preheat the oven to 150°C/300°F/Gas Mark 2.

Slice the cabbage thinly. In a large saucepan, heat the oil and sweat the onion until soft, but not brown. Add the cabbage, apples, cloves, bay leaves, sugar and vinegar and stir well for a few minutes. Add the water and bring to a gentle boil. Season well with salt and pepper and transfer everything to a lidded casserole dish.

Cook in the oven for about 1 ½ hours, checking the water level every 30 minutes or so and adding more if needed. It shouldn't be swimming in liquid, but there definitely should be some juices at the bottom. It is done when the cabbage is tender and there is an aromatic richness taking over the whole of your home.

You can freeze this for up to 1 month.

The ham

I will admit to being terrified by the concept of "The Ham" for many years. It all looked a bit big and involved. All that soaking and roasting and basting and studding. When I actually got round to doing it, the whole procedure was, inevitably, a doddle and the result so delicious I gave myself a slap round the chops for being so lily livered. Clearly, the quality of the meat you buy will impact on the deliciousness of this dish ... spare a thought for the pig.

✳ Serves 10 greedy people

4 kg/8 lb 13 oz boneless gammon
  (ham), ask your butcher to
  bone it for you
1 onion, cut in half
1 tsp black peppercorns
3 bay leaves
1 star anise
about 20 cloves
4 tbsp runny honey
1 tbsp dark soy sauce
2 tbsp dark soft brown sugar
1 tbsp English mustard (powder
  is best)

I always start by weighing the ham and writing down the actual weight. Put the piece of meat in a large pan and cover with cold water. Bring to the boil and simmer for 10 minutes. Drain it and throw away the water. Put it back in the pan, this time with the onion, peppercorns, bay leaves and star anise and cover again with cold water. Cover the pan and bring to the boil, then turn it down to a gentle simmer and cook for 25 minutes per 450 g/1 lb. (You are looking at about 3 hours for a 4 kg/8 lb 13 oz piece of meat. That's why I write down the weight...) When the meat is cooked through, take it out of the pan (but keep the liquor – makes excellent soup and risottos) and drain well.

Preheat the oven to 180°C/350°F/Gas Mark 4.

When the ham is cool enough to handle, cut off the skin, leaving behind a good layer of fat. Score the fat in a criss-cross pattern and pop a clove into each diamond. Mix together the honey, soy sauce, sugar and mustard and brush this mixture over the top of the ham, then pop it back into the oven for about 30 minutes until golden, shiny and irresistible. Serve hot, warm or cold. This beastie is good for mass catering – easy to carve and completely versatile.

Proper nut roast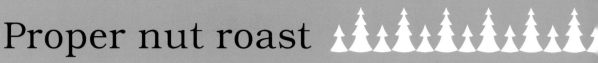

This is the nut roast I used to make regularly when I was a non-meat eater. It goes so well with all the traditional accompaniments to a roast dinner. Vary the nuts to include your favourites – a mixture is good. Chuck in other herbs and spices. It's a very forgiving recipe. Make an Onion and Marsala gravy (see p.48) to go with it and by George, you've got a good feast.

*Serves 8 quite greedy people

50 g/1¾ oz/3½ tbsp butter, plus extra for greasing
200 g/7 oz/1⅓ cups Brazil nuts (or other nuts of your choice)
1 large onion, finely chopped
2 celery sticks, finely chopped
200 g/7 oz cooked, peeled, ready to use chestnuts, roughly chopped
1 large free-range egg
120 g/4½ oz/2¼ cups fresh breadcrumbs
2 tsp chopped sage
1 tsp chopped thyme
1 tbsp chopped parsley
1 tbsp dried cranberries
finely grated zest of 1 lemon
1 tsp Marmite or yeast extract
250 ml/9 fl oz/generous 1 cup vegetable stock
salt and freshly ground black pepper

Preheat the oven to 180°C/350°F/Gas Mark 4. Grease and line the base and sides of a 700-g/1-lb 9-oz loaf tin.

Put the nuts onto a baking tray and roast in the oven for 10 minutes, or until golden brown. You can also do this in a dry frying pan (skillet) on the stove. Watch them like a hawk. Burnt nuts are disgusting. When they are all golden, chop roughly into large chunks rather than a fine mixture.

Melt the butter in a large saucepan and gently sweat the onion and celery for about 10 minutes until everything is soft and translucent. Then throw in the chopped nuts, chestnuts, egg, breadcrumbs, herbs, cranberries and lemon zest and mix well.

Stir the Marmite or yeast extract into the stock until it dissolves, then slowly add the liquid to the nut mixture, stirring as you go. Stop adding the stock as soon as the mixture forms a cohesive ... well ... sludge. (Sorry, terrible description of something delicious.) Season with salt (if needed) and pepper.

Put the mixture into the prepared tin, smooth the surface and pop into the oven for about 1 hour until golden on top and firm to the touch. Leave to cool for about 5 minutes before inverting the tin onto a serving dish and peeling back the lining paper to reveal your scrumptious nut roast.

Onion and Marsala gravy

This is a vegetarian gravy that you can make in advance and store for a few days quite happily in the refrigerator until you need to use it.

* Serves 8

2 large onions, finely chopped
1 tbsp olive oil
1 tbsp plain (all-purpose) flour
100 ml/3½ fl oz/generous ⅓ cup
   Marsala
1 tsp Marmite or yeast extract
200 ml/7 fl oz/generous ¾ cup
   vegetable stock
1 tsp redcurrant jelly
1 tsp soy sauce

In a large pan, cook the onions in the oil, stirring every now and again until the onions are really brown. Don't try and skimp on the brownness – it is this that gives the gravy its wonderful flavour. When the onions are a deep golden colour, add the flour and stir it around for about 1 minute. Add the Marsala all in one go and stir away. Inhale the heady fumes and enjoy.

Dissolve the Marmite or yeast extract in the stock and slowly add this to the pan, stirring well before adding any more stock. Add the redcurrant jelly and melt this in. Let the gravy simmer gently for about 10 minutes to cook out the flour and let everything thicken slightly. Stir it every now and again, then taste. Instead of adding salt, I add a small slug of soy sauce. It adds saltiness, depth and helps turn the gravy a delicious rich brown. Yum. When you are happy with the consistency and flavour, strain the gravy through a sieve into a warm jug and serve.

Bread sauce

I can't imagine Christmas lunch without bread sauce. It would be so wrong. Almost as wrong as packet bread sauce. Now, that is wrong. Proper bread sauce is criminally easy and so scrumptious you dream about bathing in it. Oh, just me then?

* Serves 8

6 cloves
1 onion, peeled
600ml/1 pint/2½ cups whole milk (plus some extra)
1 bay leaf
6 black peppercorns
1 small white loaf (at least one day old)
salt and freshly ground black pepper
freshly grated nutmeg (optional)

Stud the cloves into the onion and place into a saucepan with 600 ml/1 pint/2½ cups milk, the bay leaf and peppercorns. Bring to the boil then turn the heat off immediately and leave the milk to infuse for about half an hour.

Meanwhile, turn the loaf into breadcrumbs – a food processor is by far the easiest method. You could do it by hand, but I'd be inclined to remove the crusts if you do it this way.

Strain the milk into another saucepan and discard the onion and all it's flavoursome friends. Add the breadcrumbs to the milk and let it sit happily until you need it. To reheat the sauce, add a little milk if it is too thick then put the saucepan back over a gentle heat, stirring to stop it sticking until it is warm. Check for seasoning and add a little freshly grated nutmeg if you like that sort of thing.

Venison stew

I think venison is a lovely meat and the great thing about serving something like a very special venison stew at Christmas is that it really does need to be made several days in advance. This leaves Christmas morning stress-free on the culinary front, allowing you to concentrate on arranging your facial expression into something appropriate when you are handed a present of such vileness your immediate thought is to throw an unseasonal tantrum.

✳ Serves 8

1.5 kg/3 lb 5 oz cubed shoulder
  of venison

For the marinade
2 bottles red wine
1 large onion, sliced
5 tbsp olive oil
3 bay leaves
1 large rosemary sprig
3 thyme sprigs
6 juniper berries
6 garlic cloves, peeled
salt and freshly ground black
  pepper

For the stew
4 tbsp plain (all-purpose) flour
  seasoned with salt and pepper
olive oil, for frying
200 g/7 oz lardons (small pieces
  of diced bacon)
2 large onions, chopped
2 large carrots, peeled and cut
  into chunks
  (list continues opposite)

First, make your marinade by putting all the ingredients in a large bowl. Tip in the venison and turn it around in the mixture so that all the meat is covered. Cover the bowl tightly with clingfilm (plastic wrap) and leave in the refrigerator for 24 hours.

Preheat the oven to 150°C/130°F/Gas Mark 2.

Drain the meat from the marinade – keep the marinade – and dry the venison on clean tea towels or kitchen paper (paper towels), then dust lightly in the seasoned flour.

In a large frying pan (skillet), heat the oil and fry the lardons until crispy and brown. Remove from the pan and put them in a large casserole dish. Brown the venison in batches in the bacon fat, putting the browned meat with the lardons in the casserole dish as you go. Brown the vegetables (apart from the dried mushrooms) and add them to the meat.

Deglaze the pan with the strained marinade and tip it over the meat. Add enough stock to cover the meat and vegetables, put the lid on and cook in the oven for at least 2 hours.

2 celery sticks, chopped
40 g/1 ½ oz mixed dried
   mushrooms
500 ml/18 fl oz/generous 2 cups
   beef stock

Meanwhile, put the dried mushrooms in a heatproof bowl. Boil the kettle and pour enough boiling water over the mushrooms to cover then leave them to soak.

After the first hour of the stew's cooking time, remove from the oven and add the soaked mushrooms, adding the soaking liquor too, but make sure you leave behind any grit which sometimes clings to the mushrooms. Put the casserole back in the oven for another hour and then test the meat for tenderness. You may wish to put it back for a further 30 minutes or so.

My advice at this stage would be to leave the stew well alone in a cool place (refrigerator or cold larder if you have one) for 2 days – it is always better. On the day you want to eat it, heat it in the oven at 160°C/140°F/Gas Mark 3 for about an hour and check the sauce for seasoning.

Eat with all the usual Christmas accompaniments. Gorgeous.

Desserts

4

This is a chapter to be taken seriously indeed. There are several theories flying around, which certainly seem to stand up to investigation, particularly where children are concerned: we have two stomachs – a first course stomach and a dessert stomach. One can be stuffed to the brim with roast potatoes and turkey, but mysteriously, when dessert is presented, the second stomach desperately needs filling (with several helpings). What luck!

The traditional Christmas pudding appears to split the nation. You love it or loathe it. I've included the über traditional recipe, which should be made weeks in advance and a quick last minute one for people (like me) who forget. There are lots of other celebratory desserts for those who think they are full but might manage a wafer-thin slice of something light and chocolatey, or perhaps creamily soft, or perhaps a little bit alcoholic, or perhaps slightly fruity. Go on then, a little bit of everything – it is Christmas.

Christmas pudding

You can make this traditional Christmas pudding up to two months in advance, and store it in a cool, dark place. Quite frankly, if you are that organized, I worry, I really do. I reckon a month is quite adequate and more normal (and really organized, in my world). Feel free to change the fruits, nuts and alcohol to suit your tastes.

❋ Serves 8

125 g/4½ oz/generous ¾ cup currants
125 g/4½ oz/scant ¾ cup sultanas (golden raisins)
125 g/4½ oz/¾ cup raisins
75 g/2¾ oz dates, pitted and chopped
75 g/2¾ oz dried figs, chopped
finely grated zest and juice of 1 orange
75 ml/2½ fl oz/5 tbsp brandy or rum, plus a little extra to serve (optional)
butter, for greasing
50 g/1¾ oz shredded vegetarian suet
50 g/1¾ oz/⅓ cup self-raising (self-rising) flour
75 g/2¾ oz/1½ cups soft white breadcrumbs
½ tsp mixed spice
1 tsp ground cinnamon
½ tsp ground cloves
½ tsp ground allspice
100 g/3½ oz/½ cup dark soft brown sugar
(list continues opposite)

Start by putting the dried fruit into a large bowl (not metal) and cover with the fruit juice, zest and the brandy or rum. Cover with clingfilm (plastic wrap) and leave overnight for all the liquid to soak into the fruit.

The next day, grease a 1-litre/1¾-pint/1-quart pudding basin (ovenproof bowl) with butter and put a disc of greaseproof (wax) paper into the base.

Get your bowl of tipsy fruit, add in all the other ingredients, then stir really well. How easy is that? Spoon the mixture into the prepared pudding basin and press down well. It doesn't rise much, so don't worry if it comes to nearly the top of the basin.

Cut out a 38-cm/15-in square of baking parchment and a piece of foil of the same size and lay the foil on top of the parchment. Make a pleat of 4 cm/1½ in down the centre of both pieces and put this, foil side up, over the top of the basin, smoothing down the sides of the square over the bowl. Tie a long piece of string around the bowl, just under the lip, to secure all in place. You can make a snazzy little handle out of extra string if you want, at this point, by bringing it

25 g/1 oz almonds, roughly
  chopped
1 medium-sized apple, unpeeled,
  grated
2 large free-range eggs, beaten

over the top of the bowl and tying it to the string on the other side of the bowl.

In a deep saucepan with a tight-fitting lid, put a little trivet or an upturned saucer (that won't crack in boiling water) in the base and place the basin carefully on top. Pour in enough water to come halfway up the bowl and put the lid on. Bring the pan to simmering point and cook for 5 hours. Keep checking the water level and top it up as needed.

After the allotted time, remove the bowl from the pan and leave to cool. As soon as it is cool, wrap the basin in cling film and then a layer of foil and it is then ready to store until needed.

To reheat the pudding, remove the foil and clingfilm, but leave the original top covering on. Pop the basin into the pan of water as you did for the initial cooking and steam for 2 hours. Take the top covering off, run a knife around the pudding and turn it out onto a plate. If you are feeling brave and have a fire extinguisher to hand, feel free to gently heat a small amount of brandy or rum, pour it over the pudding and ignite. Laugh nervously as the flames leap towards the paper chains...

A sneaky last-minute Christmas pudding

This really can be made in minutes. You could easily make it on Christmas morning with no stress at all and put it on to steam when the turkey goes in. The secret here is to use mincemeat. If you use shop-bought, get the best you can – a luxury jar will make all the difference. Feel free to jazz it up with a small handful of nuts or some extra dried fruit such as cranberries.

✳Serves 8

butter, for greasing
600 g/1 lb 5 oz mincemeat
  (homemade see p.17 or
  shop-bought)
finely grated zest of 1 orange
60 ml/2 fl oz/4 tbsp brandy
50 g/1¾ oz/⅓ cup self-raising
  flour
50 g/1¾ oz/1 cup fresh white
  breadcrumbs
1 tsp mixed spice
1 tsp ground cinnamon
½ tsp ground ginger
1 large free-range egg

Grease a 1-litre/1¾-pint/1-quart ovenproof pudding bowl with butter and line the base with greaseproof (wax) paper.

Put all the ingredients into a large bowl and stir everything together well. Tip the mixture into the prepared pudding basin. Cut a large square of baking parchment and a same size piece of foil and lay the foil on top of the parchment. Make a pleat in the centre of both pieces and put this, foil side up, over the top of the basin, smoothing down the edges. Tie a piece of string around the basin, just under the lip.

Put a trivet or an upturned saucer (that won't crack in boiling water) in the base of a deep saucepan with a tight-fitting lid and place the basin carefully on top. Pour in enough water to come halfway up the bowl and put the lid on. Bring the pan to simmering point and cook for 3½ hours. Keep an eye on the water and top it up as and when needed.

Carefully remove the pudding from the pan, take the foil and parchment lid off, slide a knife around the pudding and turn it out onto a plate. This is a gorgeous Christmas pudding. And a superb vehicle for cream or Brandy butter (p.16)...

Orange cake with lemon posset

Sometimes a dessert is required that cuts through the richness of Christmas dinner. A burst of citrus is just the thing. This light cake, served in thin, elegant slices with a tiny glass of lemon posset to accompany it, is a grown-up pudding. There's no alcohol, there's no dried fruit, there are no scary spices, but it's still grown up.

✳ Serves 10

For the cake
225 g/8 oz/1 cup unsalted butter, plus extra for greasing
225 g/8 oz/1⅛ cups caster (superfine) sugar
225 g/8 oz/2½ cups ground almonds
3 large free-range eggs
110 g/3½ oz/generous ⅔ cup polenta (cornmeal)
zest and juice of 3 oranges
½ tsp baking powder
80 g/3 oz/scant ½ cup caster sugar
juice of 1 lemon

For the posset
600 ml/1 pint/2½ cups double (heavy) cream
150 g/5½ oz/⅔ cup caster sugar
juice of 2 large lemons

Make the posset first. Put the cream and sugar into a large pan and bring to the boil. Boil for about 3 minutes then remove from the heat and whisk in the lemon juice. Strain the mixture into a jug and then pour into 10 dainty glasses or bowls that will look good next to the cake. Pop them into the refrigerator for about 4 hours.

Now for the cake. Preheat the oven to 160°C/315°F/Gas Mark 2–3 and grease and base-line a 20-cm/8-in loose-bottomed cake tin with baking parchment.

Cream together the butter and sugar until really pale and fluffy (I use a freestanding mixer). Add 1 tbsp of the ground almonds and beat in, then add the eggs, one at a time, beating really well before adding the next one. Fold in the remaining almonds, the polenta (cornmeal), orange zest and baking powder.

Put the mixture into the prepared tin and bake for about 45 minutes, or until a skewer inserted into the middle of the cake comes out clean. Leave the cake in its tin.
(continues on p.61)

While the cake is cooking, make the orange syrup, which gives the cake that gorgeous, sticky hit of citrus. Put the remaining caster (superfine) sugar and the citrus juices into a small pan and boil the mixture vigorously until all the sugar has dissolved and you have a thin syrup.

Take the cake out of the oven and prick it all over with a skewer about 20 times. Pour the syrup over the surface of the cake so that it soaks in to the warm sponge and leave the cake to soak up all the lovely syrup until it is completely cold.

Remove the cake from the tin just before serving. Serve with the posset on the side.

Pannacotta with mulled wine syrup

Pannacotta is a wonderful dessert – easy to eat, gently reassuring, yet wonderfully special. The mulled wine syrup, served neither hot, nor cold, but at blood temperature give this pudding a gorgeous, velvety, Christmassy hug.

✳ Serves 6

150 ml/5 fl oz/⅔ cup whole milk
425 ml/15 fl oz/scant 2 cups double (heavy) cream
85 g/3 oz/scant ½ cup caster (superfine) sugar
1 vanilla pod (bean)
4 sheets (6.5 g) leaf gelatine (not powdered)
4 tbsp very hot water

For the syrup
500 ml/18 fl oz/generous 2 cups red wine
100 g/3½ oz/½ cup caster sugar
2 cloves
2 star anise
1 cinnamon stick
1 orange, cut in half
lemon juice, to taste (optional)

Put the milk, cream and sugar into a saucepan and split the vanilla pod (bean) lengthways down the middle. Scrape out the seeds with the point of a knife into the pan with the milk and fling the vanilla pod in as well. Heat until the mixture comes to the boil then turn off the heat and let everything infuse together for about 30 minutes.

Pop the gelatine sheets into a flat dish, cover with cold water and leave them for about 5 minutes to become spongy. Squeeze out the gelatine and put them into a bowl with the very hot water. Stir until the gelatine has dissolved then add 4 tbsp of the milk mixture and stir away. Tip the whole lot into the rest of the milky mixture and whisk it really well. Pass the mixture through a sieve (strainer) into a jug then pour it into 6 ramekins or dariole moulds. Cover with clingfilm (plastic wrap) and leave them to set in the refrigerator for at least 4 hours.

To make the syrup, put all the ingredients (except the lemon juice) into a saucepan and bring to the boil. Keep boiling until the mixture has reduced by half and you should end up with a very deep red, syrup – almost like a cordial. Taste the syrup (when it is cool enough) and add some lemon juice if you think it needs it. Strain the syrup into a jug and serve with the pannacotta.

Christmas trifle

This is a complete invention that has sort of morphed from a syllabub into a posset and then into trifle. It is boozy, lemony, creamy, crunchy and the most sinfully easy dessert you could ever wish for. Make it in individual glasses or one large trifle bowl – it will make you whimper with joy.

✳ Serves 8

150 g/5½ oz amaretti or rataffia
  biscuits (cookies), broken up
  into chunks
100 ml/3½ fl oz/generous ⅓ cup
  dry sherry
2 x 425 g/15 oz can pitted black
  cherries
2 tbsp quark
2 tbsp crème fraîche
3 tbsp lemon curd
200 g/7 oz ready-made custard
2 tbsp flaked (slivered) almonds,
  toasted

Put the chunks of biscuits (cookies) into the bases of 8 individual glasses or a large trifle bowl and sprinkle over 50 ml/1¾ fl oz/scant ¼ cup sherry. Top with a layer of cherries.

In a separate bowl, mix together the quark, crème fraîche, lemon curd and custard until smooth and unctuous. Slowly add the remaining 50 ml/1¾ fl oz/scant ¼ cup sherry, tasting the mixture after adding about a half of the sherry and seeing if you want to continue! I always do, but that may say more about myself than the actual dessert. When you are happy, pour the mixture on top of the cherries and finally scatter the toasted flaked (slivered) almonds on top. Chill until needed – it will happily stay in the refrigerator for a day.

Panettone bread and butter pudding

Bread and butter pudding? I love you. Panettone? I love you too. You know the bit in the church where the vicar says, " If anyone knows a just cause or impediment...?" No one stood up. The marriage occurred and all the dessert-eaters lived happily ever after.

✳ Serves 8

50 ml/1¾ fl oz/scant ¼ cup brandy
75 g/2¾ oz/½ cup raisins
butter, for greasing
700 g/1 lb 9 oz panettone
4 large free-range eggs
50 g/1¾ oz/¼ cup caster (superfine) sugar
300 ml/10 fl oz/1¼ cups whole milk
300 ml/10 fl oz/1¼ cups double (heavy) cream
1 vanilla pod (bean)
3 tbsp apricot jam

First, warm the brandy in a pan and tip in the raisins. Take the pan off the heat and let the raisins plump up in the brandy for about 2 hours.

Preheat the oven to 150°C/300°F/Gas Mark 2 and generously grease a baking dish with butter.

Cut the panettone into slices about 2 cm/¾ in thick and layer them in the prepared dish, scattering in the brandy raisins as you go. Press the panettone down into the dish.

In a separate bowl, lightly whisk the eggs and sugar together. Pour the milk and cream into a pan and split the vanilla pod (bean) lengthways down the middle. Scrape out the seeds with the point of a knife into the pan with the milk and cream and fling in the vanilla pod too. Bring the mixture to the boil and immediately remove the pan from the heat. While whisking, pour the hot liquid onto the egg and sugar mixture then pass the mixture through a sieve (strainer) into a jug. This removes any stringy eggy bits and of course, the vanilla pod.

Put the panettone-filled baking dish into a roasting tin and pour the jug of vanilla custard all over the panettone, making sure that all the bready cake is thoroughly covered and wallowing. Carefully slide the roasting dish into the oven. It is at this stage that I fill the roasting tin with water – there's a mass slopping if I do it earlier. You want the water to come about halfway up the baking dish.

Bake for about 30–40 minutes – the pudding should have taken on some colour on the top, be firm to the touch but still have a slight wobble in the centre. Take the whole caboodle carefully out of the oven and remove the pudding dish from its water bath and leave to cool.

When the pudding is cool, pass the apricot jam though a sieve so that it is utterly smooth into a small pan. Warm the jam and then brush it all over the top of the pudding.

This is dessert is best eaten at room temperature. Crikey, it's good.

Chocolate nougat mousse

Should I apologize for another massively easy recipe? If you are cross with me: I am very sorry. May I suggest you go and make some Stollen (see p.86). I, for one, don't really want to be making really complicated desserts after the whole roast turkey caboodle. But I want the dessert to be really, really delicious. Like this.

* Serves 6

295 g/10¼ oz bar Toblerone or other nougat chocolate, chopped into chunks
6 tbsp boiling water
2 tsp very strong espresso coffee
275 ml/9½ fl oz/scant 1¼ cups crème fraîche
2 large free-range egg whites
chocolate chunks, shavings or sprinkles, to decorate (optional)
crispy biscuits (cookies) of your choice, to serve

Put the chocolate, boiling water and coffee into a heatproof bowl set over a pan of barely simmering water. The base of the bowl must not touch the water. Let the chocolate melt really slowly and when melted, stir the chocolate gently to incorporate all the ingredients. Let the chocolate cool and thicken.

When the chocolate has thickened, fold in the crème fraîche. Whisk the egg whites in a clean grease-free bowl until they reach firm peaks then fold into the mixture – I do this in 3 batches.

Spoon the mousse into whatever receptacle you wish to serve it in, such as individual bowls, glasses or one large bowl, it's up to you, and chill for at least 2 hours before serving. Scatter the tops with chocolate shavings or sprinkles, if wished and serve with a crispy biscuit.

Chestnut cheesecake

"Chestnuts roasting on an open fire, la la laaaaaaa" ... anyway ... have you ever tried roasting chestnuts on an open fire? Absolutely terrifying. They explode and shards of molten chestnut come careering towards your eyes at 200mph. Should be a law against it. Chestnuts are Christmassy, but we can do without a trip to hospital. Luckily this recipe calls for a can of chestnut purée. This cheesecake is my salute to the classic French dessert of chestnuts and cream – *Mont Blanc*. You can get crystallized (candied) chestnuts from good delis.

❋ Serves 8

200 g/7 oz digestive biscuits (graham crackers), crushed to crumbs
100 g/3½ oz/7 tbsp unsalted butter, melted
250 g/9 oz canned sweetened chestnut purée
300 g/10 oz/1⅓ cups cream cheese
300 ml/10 fl oz/1¼ cups double (heavy) cream, whipped
2 tbsp crème fraîche
150 g/5½ oz crystallized (candied) chestnuts, roughly chopped
(unsweetened) cocoa powder, grated dark chocolate, dragees or crystallized (candied) chestnuts, to decorate

Line a 20-cm/8-in loose-bottomed cake tin with clingfilm (plastic wrap), making sure that the clingfilm comes right over the top of the tin.

Tip the crushed biscuits into the melted butter and stir well to incorporate. Put the biscuit mixture into the base of the tin and press it down really firmly with the back of a spoon. Put the tin in the refrigerator for about 1 hour to allow the base to firm up.

In a large bowl, beat together the chestnut purée and cream cheese. Carefully fold in the whipped cream and crème fraîche until everything is completely smooth, then add the chestnuts and fold them in as well. Spoon the gorgeous mixture onto the biscuit base and smooth the top. Chill in the refrigerator for at least 6 hours (overnight is even better).

To finish it off, push the base out and ease the cheesecake out of the tin. The clingfilm should peel away from the sides. Slide a palette knife under the base and move the whole to a serving plate. Top with a dusting of cocoa, some shavings of dark chocolate, dragees or slivers of crystallized chestnut.

Large cakes for gorging 5

You have to have a Christmas cake of some sort. Don't you? Surely? There has to be that uncomfortable moment late on Christmas Day afternoon when you have collapsed into the sofa and don't have the strength to show any enthusiasm for the Scrabble set which is being waved in front of you. Some smart alec then pipes up with "Anyone fancy a cup of tea and a bit of cake?"

Suddenly this seems like the worst idea and the best idea all at the same time. You perk up enormously when the teapot arrives and a plate bearing a massive cake.

It might not be right, but you know it's true. The other thing to remember is that a traditional fruit Christmas cake lasts for months, so it isn't a waste if you only pick at it a bit on Christmas day.

Other Christmas cakes might not have the longevity of the fruit, but there isn't a rule that says you can only eat a Yule log on Christmas day. The fantastic run up to Christmas and the post Christmas gloom all require cake. And that is a real rule. I've checked.

The proper Christmas cake

I refuse to re-invent the wheel. This is a fantastic fruitcake recipe, given to me by my lovely friend James and it has appeared in *Cake Magic*. It is the best recipe I have come across and I adore it. This recipe makes two – give one as a present if you can bear to. You will score many points with the recipients.

✳ **Makes 2 cakes**

900 g/2 lb dried fruit (raisins, sultanas, currants, cranberries)
100 g/3½ oz glacé (candied) cherries, halved
50 g/1¾ oz glacé (candied) cherries, whole
150 ml/5 fl oz/⅔ cup alcohol (brandy, rum, port, Marsala or a mixture)
200 g/7 oz/⅞ cup unsalted butter, plus extra for greasing
200 g/7 oz/1 cup dark soft brown sugar
2 tbsp black treacle (blackstrap molasses)
1 tbsp golden syrup (dark corn syrup)
1 tbsp thick cut marmalade
1 tsp vanilla extract
225 g/8 oz/scant 1⅔ cups plain (all-purpose) flour
2 tsp mixed spice
1 tsp ground cloves
2 tsp ground cinnamon
pinch of salt
4 large free-range eggs
(list continues opposite)

The day before baking, soak all the dried fruit in the alcohol.

The next day, preheat the oven to 150°C/300°F/Gas Mark 2 and grease and line 2 x 15-cm/6-in cake tins, preferably with loose bottoms, with baking parchment.

Cream together the butter and sugar until really fluffy then add the treacle (molasses), syrup, marmalade and vanilla and beat it thoroughly to make sure all the ingredients are mixed in. Sift the flour, spices and salt onto the mixture and mix it in really well. Add the eggs, one by one, mixing well before adding the next. Tip in the bowl of tipsy fruit along with any leftover liquid and mix in, then stir in the nuts.

Divide the mixture between the prepared cake tins and smooth the tops. Make a slight dent in the centre of each cake with the back of a spoon. Take a double layered piece of brown wrapping paper just over the circumference of each tin, and 4 cm/1½ in higher, and wrap it around each tin securing with string. This helps to keep the sides of the cake from scorching and for 3 minutes of faffing, it makes all the difference.

Bake the cakes for about 3 hours (this really depends on the size of your tins – if you are making 1 whopper, it will take

100 g/3½ oz/⅔ cup almonds,
   roughly chopped
50 g/1¾ oz/⅓ cup Brazil nuts,
   roughly chopped
25 g/1 oz/scant ¼ cup whole
   hazelnuts

To decorate
4 tbsp apricot jam, sieved
icing (confectioners') sugar,
   for dusting
1 kg/2 lb 4 oz marzipan
   (homemade, see p.11, or
   shop-bought)
1 batch royal icing (see p.10)

longer or for 4 littlies, not as long). The cakes are cooked when a skewer inserted into the cakes comes out clean. If the tops are overbrowning, but the cakes aren't done, put some baking parchment over the top.

After you have removed the cakes from the oven, leave to cool in the tins then remove to a wire rack to cool. Pierce the top of each cake with a skewer about 10 times and pour about 3 tbsp of alcohol over, then quickly put the cakes into a plastic bag, and then into an airtight tin.

Every week or so "feed" the cakes with a spoonful or two of alcohol.

About a week before you want to eat the cakes, remove them from their bags and place on 2 cake boards. Brush all over the top and sides of the cakes with a thin layer of sieved apricot jam.

Sprinkle a little icing (confectioners') sugar onto a work surface and roll out the marzipan to about 3 mm/⅛ in thick. Carefully roll it over your rolling pin, transfer it to the cake and smooth the marzipan over the cake, working from the centre towards the edges and then down the sides. Trim the excess marzipan from the base of the cake and wave goodbye to it for 24 hours. Repeat with the other cake. Leave the cakes, uncovered, somewhere cool and quiet (they are resting).

The next day, put the cakes, royal icing and a palette knife in front of you. Stare at the cakes, gird your loins and smother each one with the icing. You can make it smooth or spiky, it's up to you. Go for it. Decorate at will with edible or non-edible decorations and leave the snowy creations for at least 48 hours to dry before tucking in.

Last-minute
Christmas cake

Hands up all those who have realized that there is less than a week
until Christmas and the cake that you promised to make hasn't
actually ... been made. Do not fret, my forgetful chums. This is a beauty
and no one need ever know. If it is truly last minute, don't bother icing
it – brush some apricot jam over the top and plonk on some delicious,
jewel-like candied fruits. If you do want to ice it, follow the instructions
for the traditional Christmas cake on p.74.

* Makes 1 cake

750 g/1 lb 10 oz mixed dried fruit
  (raisins, sultanas/golden
  raisins, candied peel,
  cranberries, currants –
  whatever mixture you like)
150 g/5½ oz glacé (candied)
  cherries
225 ml/8 fl oz/1 cup apple juice
  or cider
100 ml/3½ fl oz/generous ⅓ cup
  port or brandy, plus extra for
  drizzling (optional)
75 ml/2¾ fl oz/5 tbsp orange
  juice
finely grated zest of 1 orange
2 tbsp black treacle (blackstrap
  molasses)
200 g/7 oz/⅞ cup butter, plus
  extra for greasing
200 g/7 oz/1 cup dark soft brown
  sugar
      (list continues opposite)

First, put all the dried fruit, together with the cherries,
apple juice or cider, port or brandy, orange juice and zest
and treacle (molasses) into a large pan and bring the
mixture to a fast boil. Turn the heat down and simmer for
15 minutes then turn the heat off and let the mix cool.
If you can leave it overnight, all the better, but I am thinking
you may be in more of a rush, so just leave it for as long
as you can.

Preheat the oven to 140°C/275°F/Gas Mark 1 and grease
and line a 20-cm/8-in loose-bottomed heavy cake tin with
baking parchment.

Put all the ingredients apart from the soaked fruit and nuts
into a freestanding mixer and give it a jolly good thrashing.
If you are using a wooden spoon and elbow grease approach,
just make sure everything is mixed in really well. Mix in
the fruit, any remaining liquid and the nuts, then spoon the
mixture into the prepared tin, smooth the top and make a
small dent in the centre with the back of a spoon.

250 g/9 oz/generous 1¾ cups
   plain (all-purpose) flour
1 tsp baking powder
5 large free-range eggs
2 tsp mixed spice
1 tsp ground cinnamon
100 g/3½ oz/⅔ cup nuts,
   roughly chopped (almonds,
   walnuts, Brazils, pecans,
   hazelnuts are all good)

To decorate (optional)
3 tbsp apricot jam
candied fruits
450 g/1 lb marzipan (homemade,
   see p.11, or shop-bought)
1 batch royal icing (see p.10)

As with the traditional Christmas cake baking approach (see p.74), I like to wrap the tin in a double band of brown wrapping paper and secure it with string. This really does help stop the sides of the cake scorching. Bake for about 3 hours, but check after 2½ hours. It is cooked when a skewer inserted into the middle of the cake comes out clean. You may need to cover the top of the cake with baking parchment if it is getting too brown before the cake is fully cooked.

Leave the cake to cool completely in the tin. If you wanted to add some extra oomph to the proceedings, you could pierce the top with a skewer about 10 times and drizzle in 2 tbsp port or brandy. I'm sure no one would mind. Brush the surface with apricot jam and decorate with candied fruits or marzipan and icing.

Gingerbread house of fun

Making a gingerbread house may look daunting, but believe me, with my easy instructions and a wee nip of the cooking sherry, anything is possible.

✳ Makes 1 house with enough
   spare gingerbread to make
   biscuits (cookies) too

675 g/1 lb 7 oz/generous 4¾ cups
   plain (all-purpose) flour (plus
   extra for dusting)
1½ tsp bicarbonate of soda
   (baking soda)
2 tbsp ground ginger
1 tbsp ground cinnamon
1 tsp ground allspice
175 g/6 oz/¾ cup unsalted
   butter
225 g/8 oz/1⅛ cups soft light
   brown sugar
6 tbsp golden syrup (dark
   corn syrup)
1 large free-range egg
sweets (candies), to decorate

For the royal icing
250 g/9 oz/scant 2¼ cups icing
   (confectioners') sugar, sifted
1 large free-range egg white
2 tsp freshly squeezed lemon
   juice

First, get cracking on your gingerbread. Sift the flour, bicarbonate of soda (baking soda) and spices into a large bowl. Add the butter and rub it in until you have a texture resembling fine breadcrumbs. Add the sugar and mix well.

Put the syrup and egg into a warmed bowl and mix together – much easier to do it this way, believe me. Pour the wet mixture onto the dry mixture and mix to form a soft, smooth dough. I do this in my freestanding mixer with a dough hook, but you can do it by hand just as well. Wrap the dough in clingfilm (plastic wrap) and chill for at least 1 hour (2 hours is better and overnight better still).

Meanwhile, make the royal icing. Tip the icing (confectioners') sugar into a large bowl (freestanding mixer with a paddle attachment even better). Add the egg white and lemon juice and beat for at least 5 minutes. You may need to add a little cold water, if the mix is too dry and crumbly, but add it very slowly. Conversely if the mixture is too loose, add more icing sugar. After about 5 minutes of beating you should have a thick, white meringue-type mixture that holds its peak. Store in an airtight container in the refrigerator until needed.

Line several baking sheets with silicone paper. Cut templates for the house: 2 side walls (16 x 13 cm/6¼ x 5 in), 2 gable end walls (16 x 13cm/6¼ x 5 in, rising to a point in the centre of 23 cm/9 in) and 2 roof pieces (20.5 x 15.5 cm/8 x 6 in). *(continues on p.80)*

(continues on p.80)

Roll the chilled dough out on a floured work surface to a thickness of about 5 mm/¼ in and cut round the templates. Lay the pieces onto the prepared baking sheets and chill for another hour. This stops the pieces from spreading during cooking. Cut out cookie shapes from the spare dough at this stage (or freeze the dough for another day).

Preheat the oven to 180°C/350°F/Gas Mark 4.

Bake the gingerbread for 8–10 minutes, or until golden brown. As soon as they are out of the oven, put those templates on top of the hot pieces pronto and cut round the outline to make sure you have really sharp edges. You need to do this before the gingerbread cools down and crisps up. Get moving! When they have firmed up, leave to cool completely on wire racks.

I like to pipe my decorations onto the house before it is assembled. Put some of the royal icing into a piping (pastry) bag and pipe the windows, roof tiles, doors or whatever your heart desires all over the outside of the house. Then (this is important, listen up), leave them to dry overnight.

The next day, you can handle your flat pack house without smudging your piping. Pipe a thick line of royal icing down the edges of the back of the house and stick on the 2 sides. You may need an extra pair of hands here, or do what I do and prop the walls against kitchen utensils, jars, cans, etc. Then add the front wall and finally the roof panels. The icing is your cement and may be used liberally. It is snow, after all.

Add sweets, edible balls and any other intricacies that appeal. Stand back and bask in the glow of achievement. If your walls are a bit wobbly insist that they are meant to be that way and cross that person off your Christmas card list!

Panforte

Panforte is the Italian treat, traditionally eaten at Christmas. Incredibly sweet and rich, packed to the gunnels with fruit and nuts, this is the sort of thing to have in very thin slices after dinner with a cup of very dark coffee or a glass of Vin Santo.

❋ Serves 10

250 g/9 oz dried figs
½ tsp ground cinnamon
½ tsp ground cardamom
½ tsp ground cloves
½ tsp freshly grated nutmeg
50 g/1¾ oz/scant ¼ cup runny honey
100 g/3½ oz/½ cup dark soft brown sugar
50 g/1¾ oz/⅓ cup blanched almonds
50 g/1¾ oz/⅓ cup hazelnuts
50 g/1¾ oz/⅓ cup Brazil nuts, roughly chopped
250 g/9 oz candied fruit, roughly chopped (preferably from whole fruits)
4 tbsp plain (all-purpose) flour
50 ml/1¾ fl oz/scant ¼ cup Vin Santo
icing (confectioners') sugar, for dusting

Preheat the oven to 150°C/300°F/Gas Mark 2 and line the base and sides of a 20-cm/8-in square cake tin with edible rice paper. Don't even think about missing this bit out. The rice paper is eaten and is part of the joy of it. You will also never, ever, get it out of the tin if you don't use it.

Finely chop the figs and put them into a saucepan with just enough water to cover. Add the spices, honey and sugar and simmer for 10 minutes until you have a sticky, but not wet mass.

Tip the figs into a mixing bowl and add the nuts, candied fruit, flour and Vin Santo and mix really well – it will be very sticky.

Tip the mixture into the prepared tin and smooth the top. Bake for 30–40 minutes, or until it feels drier and firm to the touch. Leave the panforte to cool in the tin before turning it out and dusting the top thickly with icing (confectioners') sugar.

Galette des Rois

The cake of kings. This delicious French cake is traditionally eaten at Epiphany. A small ceramic figure is placed in the cake and whoever gets it in their slice either visits the dentist or is King or Queen. If you like almonds, you'll love this.

* Serves 6

75 g/2¾ oz/⅓ cup unsalted butter, softened
1 tsp caster (superfine) sugar
20 g/¾ oz/2 tbsp plain (all-purpose) flour, plus extra for dusting
75 g/2¾ oz/generous ¾ cup ground almonds
1 large free-range egg, beaten
1 tbsp rum
500 g/1 lb 2 oz all butter puff pastry (not ready rolled)
1 large free-range egg yolk
1 tbsp milk
sugar syrup made from boiling 2 tbsp caster sugar with 2 tbsp water until dissolved
1 ceramic figure (optional) – for goodness sake, don't use anything that might melt or choke the recipient!

Start by making the almond cream filling. Beat the butter until soft, then add the sugar and beat well. Add the flour, followed by the almonds, egg and rum, beating really well before you add the next ingredient. Chill for at least 2 hours.

Line a baking sheet with silicone paper or baking parchment.

Cut the puff pastry in half and roll out the pieces on a lightly floured work surface so that you have 2 discs of pastry about 25 cm/10 in in diameter and 4 mm/⅙ in thick. Place one disc on the baking sheet, spoon a generous dollop of the almond cream onto the disc, leaving a 5-cm/2-in border free around the edge of the disc. Pop the ceramic figure in now, if using.

Mix the egg yolk with the milk to make an egg wash and brush this around the edge of the bottom disc. Place the second disc on top and press down to firmly seal the discs together. Chill for 1 hour.

Preheat the oven to 180°C/350°F/Gas Mark 4.

Brush the chilled cake with more egg wash. Cut a scalloped edge around the cake with a sharp knife. With the tip of the knife, score a sun ray pattern on top. Bake for 40 minutes, or until richly golden. While the cake is hot, brush it liberally with the sugar syrup for a shiny finish. Leave to cool before tucking in. It is best served cold or barely warm.

Christmas chocolate cake

Four (yes four) luscious layers, sandwiched with a light, yet rich chocolate cream.

✳ Serves 10-12

200 g/7 oz/⅞ cup unsalted butter, softened, plus extra for greasing
500 g/1 lb 2 oz/2½ cups caster (superfine) sugar
4 large free-range eggs
2 tsp vanilla extract
500 g/1 lb 2 oz/3½ cups plain (all-purpose) flour
2 tsp bicarbonate of soda (baking soda)
½ tsp baking powder
½ tsp salt
300 ml/10 fl oz/1¼ cups sour cream
100 g/3½ oz/generous 1 cup (unsweetened) cocoa powder (preferably Green & Blacks) dissolved in 250 ml/9 fl oz/generous 1 cup boiling water

For the filling and frosting
350 g/12 oz/12 squares dark chocolate
100 g/3½ oz/7 tbsp unsalted butter
1 tsp vanilla extract
300 ml/10 fl oz/1¼ cups sour cream
750 g/1 lb 10 oz/6½ cups icing (confectioners') sugar, sifted
3 tbsp apricot jam, sieved

Preheat the oven to 160°C/315°F/Gas Mark 2-3. Grease and line 4 x 20-cm/8-in round sandwich tins with baking parchment.

In a mixer or food processor, beat together the butter and sugar. It won't be as light and fluffy as you would expect because of the ratio of sugar to butter but just beat it really well. Add the eggs, one at a time, and you will see the texture of the mixture improve then add the vanilla followed by the dry ingredients. Keep beating well between each addition. Beat in the sour cream, followed by the cocoa mixture.

Divide the mixture between the 4 prepared tins and bake for 25-30 minutes, or until firm and springy to the touch and a skewer inserted in the middle comes out clean. Leave the cakes to cool on wire racks.

To make the filling, melt the chocolate and butter together very slowly in a heavy-based saucepan on a low heat. Stir once melted, then pour the mixture into a mixing bowl and beat in the vanilla and sour cream. Add the sifted icing (confectioners') sugar and continue beating for 5 minutes until you have a light and gorgeous frosting.

To assemble the cake, spread a thin layer of apricot jam over one layer of sponge followed by a thin layer of the chocolate frosting. Top with another sponge and repeat the process finishing with the fourth sponge. With a palette knife carefully smooth the remaining frosting over the top and sides of the cake and leave in a cool place for a couple of hours to firm up.

Stollen

Now, there's no getting around it, this is a job that needs determination in the time department. Although stollen aren't hugely difficult, there is a certain amount of faffing and three different proving (rising) stages, which means that you can wave goodbye to half a day. Having said that, this recipe makes four loaves; they freeze well; they are amazing presents and they taste sublime. I loath candied peel so substitute dates, but if you like, do add it.

* Makes 4 loaves

500 g/1 lb 2 oz/3½ cups strong
  white bread flour, plus extra
  for dusting
4 g fast-action dried yeast
25 g/1 oz/2 tbsp caster
  (superfine) sugar
1 tsp salt
250 ml/9 fl oz/generous 1 cup
  warm milk
100 g/3½ oz/7 tbsp unsalted
  butter, melted and cooled
2 large, free-range eggs

For the filling
90 g/3¼ oz/½ cup sultanas
  (golden raisins)
50 g/1¾ oz glacé (candied) cherries
100 g/3½ oz dates, pitted and
  chopped in half
50 g/1¾ oz/½ cup flaked
  (slivered) almonds
2 tbsp rum or brandy
½ tsp ground cinnamon
125 g/4½ oz marzipan, cubed

For the almond cream
75 g/2¾ oz/⅓ cup unsalted
  butter, softened
75 g/2¾ oz/¼ cup + 2 tbsp
  caster sugar
75 g/2¾ oz/generous ¾ cup
  ground almonds
20 g/¾ oz/2 tbsp plain (all-
  purpose) flour
1 large free-range egg
1 tbsp rum or brandy

For the glaze
50 g/1¾ oz/3½ tbsp unsalted
  butter
1 tbsp brandy or rum
icing (confectioners') sugar, for
  dusting

Start by making the dough. Put the flour, yeast, sugar and salt into a large bowl and stir well. Add the warm milk, melted butter and eggs and, using a wooden spoon, mix until you have a sticky dough. It is sticky. Don't panic.

Have your bag of flour sitting next to you and scatter some on the counter. Make a little mound at one side – this is for you to flour your hands with if they get sticky. Tip the dough onto the floured surface and flour your hands. Knead for 10 minutes (look at a clock if you need to). The dough loses its stickiness remarkably quickly, but keep flouring your hands as you go, rather than flouring the work surface. After 10 minutes of kneading the dough should have changed into a smooth, silky, elastic ball. If it hasn't, you need to carry on kneading until it does. Put your back into it!

Lightly flour a bowl and put the ball of dough into it. Score the top of the ball with a deep cross and cover with a clean tea (dish) towel. Leave the dough somewhere warm and draught-free for 1½ hours.

Meanwhile, put all the ingredients for the filling, apart from the marzipan, into a bowl and stir well. The alcohol can be soaking into the fruit while you wait for the dough to prove.

You can also make the almond cream now too. It is much easier to do this in a freestanding mixer or food processor, if you have one. Beat the butter until really soft then add the sugar. Once it is all incorporated add the ground almonds and beat in. Add the flour and beat that in, then add the egg and, once incorporated, finally add the rum or brandy. Put the mixture into a container and chill until you need it.

Once the dough has had its first proving, take it out of the bowl and put it onto a floured surface. Stretch it out using your fingers until you have a large square. Scatter the filling mixture all over the square and then fold into thirds. Make a quarter turn and fold into thirds again, you should end up with a ball shape again. Put the ball back into the bowl, cover with the tea towel again and leave the dough to prove for 30 minutes. Have a cup of tea and do the crossword.

Remove the dough from the bowl and cut it into 4 pieces. These will be your 4 stollens. Make one at a time or it will all go horribly wrong.

Line 4 baking trays with baking parchment. Put 1 piece of dough, uncut side down on a floured surface. Shape it into a rectangle about 20 x 15 cm/8 x 6 in. Don't worry if some of the fruit escapes, just pop it back on top of the dough, then take a dollop of almond cream and spread a thin layer all over the dough, leaving a margin of about 2 cm/¾ in all the way round. Scatter a quarter of the chopped marzipan over the cream then take a long side and fold it into the middle of the rectangle. Take the other side and fold it over so that it just overlaps at the centre. Squish all the edges a little to seal then put it seam side down onto the prepared baking tray. Repeat with the other pieces of dough until you have 4 stollens, which should be roughly 20 x 6 cm/8 x 2½ in. Cover with the tea towel and leave to prove for 2½ hours.

Preheat the oven to 170°C/325°F/Gas Mark 3.

Bake the stollens for 25 minutes, or until golden brown and hollow sounding when you tap the bottom of the loaves.

Make a glaze by melting the butter in the brandy or rum and immediately brush this all over the loaves as soon as they come out of the oven. Then, while the glaze is still wet, liberally dust with icing (confectioners') sugar and leave the loaves to cool. Retire with a huge sense of achievement.

Yule log

This is, it has to be said, a glorified Swiss (jelly) roll. Who is complaining? No one. It's chocolatey, slightly gooey and leaves you licking your fingers. A result.

❋ Serves 8

butter, for greasing
4 large free-range eggs
100 g/3½ oz/½ cup caster (superfine) sugar
65 g/2¼ oz/½ cup self-raising (self-rising) flour
40 g/1½ oz/scant ½ cup (unsweetened) cocoa powder (preferably Green and Blacks)
300 ml/10 fl oz/1¼ cups double (heavy) cream
300 g/10½ oz/10½ squares chocolate (dark is better), broken into small chunks
425 g/15 oz canned pitted black cherries, drained and roughly chopped
icing (confectioners') sugar, for dusting

For the bark (optional)
100 g/3½ oz/3½ squares dark chocolate

Preheat the oven to 200°C/400°F/Gas Mark 6 and grease and line a 33 x 23-cm/13 x 9-in Swiss roll tin (jelly roll pan) with baking parchment.

Put the eggs and caster (superfine) sugar into a bowl and whisk until they are very pale and creamy. Sift the flour and cocoa over the mixture and carefully fold it in using a metal spoon. Please try not to bash all the air out of the mixture.

Pour the mixture into the prepared tin and gently tip it this way and that to get the mixture into the corners. Bake for 8-10 minutes, or until firm and springy to the touch.

Flip the cooked sponge onto a piece of baking parchment larger than the cake and trim the edges with a sharp knife. Score a line 2.5 cm/1 in in along the whole of one long edge. With this long edge in front of you, roll up the cake away from you, trapping the baking parchment in the roll as you go. Leave the cake until completely cold.

Meanwhile, make the ganache. Put the cream into a heavy-based saucepan and bring to just under boiling point. Take the pan off the heat and throw in the chocolate. Leave the heat of the cream to melt the chocolate for a few minutes and then stir gently – it should have formed a beautiful ganache. Leave to firm up a little.

(continues on p.90)

To make the chocolate "bark", simply melt the extra chocolate and spread it over a sheet of silicone paper. Once it has set, you can snap shards off.

When the cake is cold and the ganache firmer, unroll the cake then spread about a third of the ganache over the surface and scatter the chopped cherries over the top. Roll the cake up again, this time not trapping the paper, then spread the rest of the ganache over the surface of the cake. If you are not using the chocolate bark, use a fork to make bark-like patterns in the ganache, otherwise, put shards of bark all over the log. Finally, generously dust with icing (confectioners') sugar and you're ready to serve.

Small sweet treats

You really can't do Christmas properly without mince pies, cookies and little sweet treats. When I was small, the selection of small treats was not vast it has to be said. A box of Rover biscuits (lots of plain ones and a few creamy ones), mince pies and the inevitable box of chocolate Matchmakers. When Danish butter biscuits appeared we thought we were really living it up. Oh yes, they were from Denmark and were nestled in a their own tin and in little paper cups. Get us! Things have moved on (well, we're not in the 1970s any more) and now *Lebküchen*, sweet filo (phyllo) parcels and frangipane tarts all feature in the "ooh, I'd like to make those for Christmas" category.

When people pop round, and hauling the Christmas cake out of its tin doesn't appeal, a plate of little morsels is just the thing. They go equally well with a cup of tea as with a glass of mulled wine - at elevenses or after supper as a treat. These are versatile recipes to have in your armoury and having some of these stashed in a tin at Christmas time might well save your sanity when the doorbell goes - again.

Mince pies

A stalwart of the festivities, Christmas without mince pies doesn't bear thinking about. I get a bit of a pastry overload with a lot of mince pies – I prefer more filling to pastry, so instead of putting a full lid on mine, I cut out small shapes of pastry that sit on top of the mincemeat winking at you in a joyful manner.

✳ Makes 12

1 batch sweet pastry, chilled, see p.15
butter, for greasing
plain (all-purpose) flour, for dusting
1 jar of mincemeat (homemade, see p.17, or shop-bought)
1 free-range egg yolk
1 tbsp milk
icing (confectioners') sugar, for dusting

To serve
brandy butter (homemade, see p.16, or shop-bought)
cream

Preheat the oven to 170°C/325°F/Gas Mark 3 and grease a 12-hole bun tin (or make 1 large tart in a 25-cm/10-in loose-bottomed tart tin) with butter.

On a lightly floured work surface, roll out the pastry to about 3 mm/⅛ in thick and cut out the correct sized circles for your tins. Place the pastry discs in the tins and press down well. Gather up the remaining pastry and cut out small shapes such as stars or holly leaves.

Place a heaped teaspoon of mincemeat into each pastry case (shell), smooth out and top with the pastry shape.

Lightly beat the egg yolk and milk together and brush the surface of the pastry decoration with the egg wash. Bake for about 15 minutes, or until the top pastry is golden and the underside of the tarts are crisp. Leave to cool slightly on a wire rack and then dust with icing (confectioners') sugar. Scoff while warm with oodles of brandy butter and cream.

Hazelnut *streusel* mince pies

A variation on the traditional mince pie may be seen as sacrilege by some, but I do welcome a change now and again. I love the crunchy topping on these and the nuttiness makes these mince pies extra special. This is one I often make as a large tart – a generous slice with a huge dollop of cream is a plate that rarely gets turned down. Yummy.

Makes 12 mince pies or 1 large tart

1 batch sweet pastry, chilled, see p.15
50 g/1¾ oz/3½ tbsp unsalted butter, plus extra for greasing
plain (all-purpose) flour, for dusting
1 jar of mincemeat (homemade, see p.17, or shop-bought)
85 g/3 oz/scant ⅔ cup plain (all-purpose) flour, plus extra for dusting
50 g/1¾ oz/¼ cup demerara (raw brown) sugar
1 tsp ground cinnamon
50 g/1¾ oz/⅓ cup hazelnuts, roughly chopped
1 tbsp cold water

Preheat the oven to 170°C/325°F/Gas Mark 3 and grease either a 12-hole bun tin or a 25-cm/10-in loose-bottomed tart tin with butter.

Roll out the pastry on a lightly floured surface to about 3 mm/⅛ in and cut out the appropriate sized discs for your tin or use to line the large tin. Fill the cases (shells) with mincemeat leaving enough space at the top for the *streusel*.

To make the *streusel*, mix the flour, sugar and cinnamon together in a large bowl. Cut the butter into cubes and rub it into the dry mixture until it resembles breadcrumbs. Stir in the nuts then add the 1 tbsp cold water and stir it in. This gives the *streusel* mixture a slightly knobbly texture.

Carefully spoon the *streusel* over the top of the mincemeat and bake in the oven for 15–20 minutes, or until the *streusel* is golden brown and the pastry underneath is crisp.

Festive fondant fancies

Yum, yum, yum. And so much nicer than the ones you buy. The recipe calls for margarine because it is an all-in-one method. Please don't be sneery – it's really good. I don't do lies.

✳ Makes 16

For the cake
110 g/4 oz/½ cup soft margarine, plus extra for greasing
110 g/4 oz/generous ¾ cup self-raising (self-rising) flour, sifted
110 g/4 oz/½ cup caster (superfine) sugar
2 large free-range eggs
1 tsp vanilla extract

For the decoration
½ batch buttercream (see p.10)
500 g/1 lb 2 oz box fondant icing sugar
food colouring gel (optional)

Preheat the oven to 160°C/325°F/Gas Mark 2–3 and grease and line a 20-cm/8-in square cake tin.

Put all the cake ingredients into a food processor or freestanding mixer and turn it on. So easy. When the mixture is light and mousse-like, tip it into the prepared tin and smooth the surface. Bake for 20 minutes, or until firm and springy to the touch and a skewer inserted into the middle comes out clean. Turn the cake onto a wire rack to cool.

Meanwhile, beat the buttercream until it is lovely and soft and put it into a piping (pastry) bag with a plain nozzle (tip).

When the cake is cold, cut it into 16 squares (4 slices down and 4 slices across). Pipe a small blob of buttercream onto the centre of each square and, with the back of a teaspoon, lightly flatten the blob.

Next, make up the fondant icing according to the instructions on the box and tint it whatever colour you wish. The icing should have a thick runny quality to it.

Place the cakes, spaced apart on a wire rack sitting over a tray (you can thank me later) and lay out 16 metallic paper cases (cups). Squish the bases of the cases with splayed fingers to make them a bit more square shaped and generally wider.

Have a small bowl of cold water next to you.

Spoon the runny icing over the top of the cakes, aiming for the buttercream blob and letting the icing run over the top and sides. Although the whole of the sides do not need to be covered, make sure that the top third of the sides of the cakes are smothered in icing.

Dip your fingers in the water and pick up a cake and place it in the case – look – no icing on fingers! Then carefully squash the sides of the cake onto the case and it should stay in place. Leave to dry.

You can either adopt the "sprinkle" approach to decoration – in which case do this while the icing is still wet or go for the stripy approach in which case put some of the fondant (tinted another colour) in a piping bag and just snip the very end off. Wave the icing back and forth over the cake for an authentic looking festive fondant fancy.

Lebküchen

Lebküchen are soft, spicy German cookies that really shout Christmas at you. Make them small, rather than large, and let them mellow in a tin for at least three days. The flavours develop and they get softer – which is what you want.

✳ Makes 24–48 depending on the size of your cutters

100 g/3½ oz/generous ¼ cup runny honey
100 g/3½ oz/scant ⅓ cup golden syrup (dark corn syrup)
175 g/6 oz/scant 1 cup dark soft brown sugar
350 g/12 oz/2½ cups plain (all-purpose) flour, plus extra for dusting
½ tsp bicarbonate of soda (baking soda)
1 tsp ground cinnamon
½ tsp ground cloves
1 tsp ground ginger
½ tsp ground allspice
1 large free-range egg, beaten
finely grated zest and juice of 1 lemon

For the icing (frosting)
200 g/7 oz/1 cup caster (superfine) sugar
100 ml/3½ fl oz/generous ⅓ cup water
2 tbsp icing (confectioners') sugar

Put the honey and syrup into a saucepan and bring to the boil. Take the pan off the heat and stir in the sugar. Cool for 5 minutes.

In a separate bowl, sift in all the dry ingredients. Stir the egg and lemon juice into the syrup pan then tip the wet ingredients onto the dry ingredients and mix well until it forms a dough. Cover with clingfilm (plastic wrap) and refrigerate overnight.

The next day, preheat the oven to 180°C/350°F/Gas Mark 4. Line 2 baking sheets with silicone liners or baking parchment.

On a lightly floured work surface, roll out the dough to 5 mm/ ¼ in thick and cut out small shapes. Transfer them to the baking sheets and bake for 10–12 minutes – they are done when you press them lightly and you don't leave a finger mark.

Meanwhile, make the icing (frosting). Put the caster (superfine) sugar and water into a pan and bring to a rapid boil. Boil until it reaches 115°C/239°F (if you haven't got a sugar thermometer, the mixture forms a soft ball when dropped onto a saucer of cold water). Take the pan off the heat and mix in the icing (confectioners') sugar.

As soon as the cookies are out of the oven, brush them with the icing. If the icing starts to become grainy, pop it back on the heat and add a trickle of water. When iced, transfer the cookies to a wire rack to cool completely. When cold, put them into a tin and leave for 3 days to mellow.

Christmas cupcakes

Cupcakes at Christmas tend to be eaten by children. Lots of children avoid dried fruit and mincemeat. Do them a favour and make some cakes that will make them jump for joy, eat too many and then feel vaguely sick...

✳ Makes 12

110 g/4 oz/½ cup butter, softened
110 g/4 oz/½ cup caster (superfine) sugar
85 g/3 oz/scant ⅔ cup self-raising (self-rising) flour, sifted
2 large free-range eggs, beaten
1 tsp vanilla extract
25 g/1 oz/generous ¼ cup (unsweetened) cocoa powder, sifted
3 tbsp Nutella or other good-quality chocolate spread

For the buttercream
110 g/4 oz/½ cup unsalted butter, softened
225 g/8 oz/1½ cups icing (confectioners') sugar, sifted
1 tbsp (unsweetened) cocoa powder, sifted
1 tbsp Nutella or other good-quality chocolate spread

To decorate
75 g/2¾ oz sugarpaste
icing sugar, for dusting
edible glitter

Preheat the oven to 170°C/325°F/Gas Mark 3. Line a 12-hole muffin tin with paper cases (cups).

In a freestanding mixer or food processor, beat the butter and sugar together until light and fluffy. Beat in 1 tbsp of the flour. Add the eggs slowly and the vanilla, beating all the time, then fold in the flour and cocoa.

Spoon the batter into the cases and bake for 15–20 minutes until firm and springy to the touch. Remove the cakes from the tin and leave to cool on wire racks.

Make the buttercream by beating together the butter, icing (confectioners') sugar, cocoa and Nutella until soft and fluffy. Make the decorations by rolling out the sugarpaste on a work surface lightly dusted with icing sugar to about 4 mm/⅙ in thick. Cut out seasonal shapes – holly leaves, stars, Christmas trees, etc. Sprinkle the glitter onto a saucer. Brush the surface of the shape with water and then fling them, wet side down into the glitter. Hey presto! Glittery shapes.

To finish, take a cold cupcake and cut a cone out of the middle (as if you were making butterfly cakes). Fill the hole with a smidge of Nutella and pop the lid back on. Smother with the buttercream and top with a glittery decoration. Children with magpie tendencies will start gathering and squawking.

Brandy snaps

Brandy snaps filled with whipped cream were a real treat when we were children. Then in the 1980s it all got a bit silly with ice creams and sorbets being plonked into the, quite frankly, wrongly shaped "brandy snap basket". I say, "bring back the brandy snap". They are delicious and the stuff of treats. They contain no brandy. I know! Brilliantly bizarre.

✳ Makes 12

110 g/4 oz/½ cup unsalted butter
110 g/4 oz/½ cup caster (superfine) sugar
4 tbsp golden syrup (dark corn syrup)
110 g/4 oz/generous ¾ cup plain (all-purpose) flour, sifted
1 tbsp lemon juice
¼ tsp ground ginger
sunflower oil, for oiling
300 ml/10 fl oz/1¼ cups double (heavy) cream, softly whipped

Preheat the oven to 180°C/350°F/Gas Mark 4 and line 2 baking sheets with silicone liners.

Put the butter, sugar and syrup in a heavy-based pan and heat gently until everything is melted together. Take the pan off the heat and stir in the flour, lemon juice and ground ginger. Leave the mixture to cool a little.

Drop large tablespoons of mixture onto the prepared baking sheets, leaving masses of room, as they will spread during cooking, and bake for 5–6 minutes until lacy and golden. You will need to do this in several batches.

Meanwhile, oil as many wooden spoons as you have with a little oil.

After the brandy snaps have cooled for 1 minute, use a palette knife to lift them off the baking sheet and onto a wooden spoon handle. Roll it round the handle, then, when it is firm, slide the brandy snap off the spoon. Keep going until all the mixture is baked and furled.

When you are ready to serve the brandy snaps, fill them with softly whipped cream and scoff.

Mini chocolate pecan tarts

These super rich tarts are best made in tiny mini muffin tins. They are a bite-full of heaven, but more than two might have you puffing and blowing a bit. Topping them with a tiny bit of edible gold leaf elevates these delicacies into Christmas territory, but is entirely optional. A pecan half on top does just as well. Pecan paste can be found in good delicatessens – a trawl though the internet sometimes comes up trumps if your local deli looks blankly at you.

Makes about 40

1 batch sweet pastry, chilled,
    see p.15
butter, for greasing
plain (all-purpose) flour, for
    dusting
200 ml/7 fl oz/generous ¾ cup
    double (heavy) cream
200 g/7 oz/7 squares good
    quality dark chocolate
3 tbsp pecan paste
edible gold leaf or pecan halves,
    to decorate

Preheat the oven to 170°C/325°F/Gas Mark 3 and grease several mini muffin tins with butter.

Roll out the pastry on a lightly floured surface – you want it as thin as you can – about 2–3 mm/¹⁄₁₆–⅛ in if you can manage it. Cut discs out to fit your tins and mould the dough into the tins. Line each tiny tart with a square of baking parchment and drop in some baking (dried) beans – crucial I'm afraid.

Bake the pastry cases (shells) blind for 10–15 minutes, or until golden brown and crispy. Take the cases out of the oven and leave to cool on a wire rack.

Make the filling by heating the cream in a heavy-based saucepan to just below boiling point. Take the pan off the heat and throw in the chocolate. Leave for a few minutes before gently stirring the chocolate until it is melted. Stir in 1 tbsp of the pecan paste and leave the ganache to firm up slightly.

When the pastry cases are cold, carefully brush the inside of each case with the remaining pecan paste and leave to dry for about 5 minutes. Finally, fill the cases with the ganache – you can either spoon it in or pipe it in if you prefer. Top with a slither of edible gold leaf or a pecan half.

Frangipane tarts

I have a bit of a thing for frangipane. I absolutely adore it. At Christmas I make these and put mincemeat in the bottom (as here) but at other times of the year I might use lovely jam, or some poached apricots or a few raspberries ... you get the point. Delicious warm or cold and they keep really well in a tin.

✳ Makes about 12

1 batch sweet pastry, chilled, see p.15
butter, for greasing
plain (all-purpose) flour, for dusting
12 tsp mincemeat (homemade, see p.17, or shop-bought)
250 g/9 oz/1⅛ cups unsalted butter, softened
250 g/9 oz/1¼ cups caster (superfine) sugar
25 g/1 oz/scant ¼ cup plain (all-purpose) flour, sifted
250 g/9 oz/2¾ cups ground almonds
4 large free-range eggs
icing (confectioners') sugar, for dusting

Preheat the oven to 160°C/315°F/Gas Mark 2–3 and grease a 12-hole cupcake or tart tin with butter.

Roll out the pastry on a lightly floured work surface to about 3 mm/⅛ in thick and cut out discs to fit your tin. Place the pastry discs into the tin and dollop 1 tsp of mincemeat into each case.

Make the frangipane by beating the butter and sugar together until really pale and fluffy. Add the flour and a quarter of the ground almonds before beating again. Beat in the eggs, one by one and finish by folding in the rest of the almonds.

Spoon the mixture over the mincemeat and smooth the surface. Bake for about 20 minutes, or until the frangipane is firm and golden.

Leave to cool on a wire tray and dust with a little icing (confectioners') sugar before serving.

Chocolate and filo
nut crackers

Serve these warm or cold. Hot is dangerous – molten filling will attack. Keep your pastry sheets under a damp tea towel while you are making them and the pastry won't crack. You can substitute the hazelnuts for walnuts or almonds if you prefer.

*Makes 16

150 g/5½ oz/5½ squares good
   quality dark chocolate,
   chopped into chunks
3 tbsp crème fraiche
100 g/3½ oz/generous 1 cup
   ground almonds
50 g/1¾ oz/⅓ cup hazelnuts,
   roasted and roughly chopped
8 sheets filo (phyllo) pastry
125 g/4½ oz/9 tbsp unsalted
   butter, melted
icing (confectioners') sugar,
   for dusting

Preheat the oven to 190°C/375°F/Gas Mark 5. Line 2 baking sheets with baking parchment.

Put a heatproof bowl over a pan of barely simmering water (the base of the bowl should not touch the water). Put the chocolate and crème fraiche into the bowl and gently melt them together, stirring every now and again. Take the bowl off the pan and stir in the ground almonds followed by the hazelnuts.

Brush one sheet of filo (phyllo) pastry with melted butter then fold the sheet in half lengthways and brush the top surface with butter again. Cut the filo in half across the middle so that you have 2 smaller rectangles. Take one piece of filo and put a dessertspoon of the chocolate mixture onto it, about 2 cm/ ¾ in up from the end and leaving a 1.5 cm/⅝ in gap at each side. Try and form the mixture into a sausage shape rather than a round blob. Roll up the filo into a cylinder, pinch and very gently twist the ends to form the ends of a cracker. Don't twist too hard or you will break the pastry. Place the cracker on the prepared baking sheet and brush the surface with more melted butter. Continue until you have 16 crackers.

Bake for 10–12 minutes until golden brown and the pastry is crisp. Dust with icing (confectioners') sugar while still hot and leave to cool on a wire rack before tucking in.

Index

Page numbers in **bold** denote
an illustration

Acknowledgements

Writing a book about Christmas food has been quite extraordinarily good fun. I got to eat a ridiculous amount of celebratory food – and writing recipes based around feasting really is no hardship at all. Thank you Emily, at Pavilion! Thanks in huge quantities go to Emma Solley, who as usual, has been a joy to work with. Unflappable and never defeated, she produces beautiful picture after beautiful picture. Special thanks to my niece Kitty for agreeing to lend me some of her kitchen equipment – a serious business indeed. Jenniflower, in Exeter, a fabulous florist and seller of the most aesthetically pleasing goods: thank you for lending me your stock – again. My butchers at Darts Farm, Gerald David, who got me beautiful turkey when no one else wanted it and the best bit of gammon I have ever seen, as well as all the other meaty bits and bobs, thanks chaps. Their knowledge and skill is legendary and the meat's OK too. To my recipe testers and tasters I extend huge thanks. Especially those whose diets I trashed (names withheld...). Massive thanks to lovely Gretchen for being a really great friend, collaborator, font of all knowledge and having the world's best dining room. Finally, thank you to Tarek and Rory – even though you hate Christmas pudding.